Does the world
hate the United
States?

Does the World Hate the United States?

Does the World Hate the United States?

Other books in the At Issue series:

Does the World Hate the United States?

Andrea C. Nakaya, *Book Editor*

Bruce Glassman, *Vice President*
Bonnie Szumski, *Publisher*
Helen Cothran, *Managing Editor*

GREENHAVEN PRESS
An imprint of Thomson Gale, a part of The Thomson Corporation

Detroit • New York • San Francisco • San Diego • New Haven, Conn.
Waterville, Maine • London • Munich

For more information, contact
Greenhaven Press
27500 Drake Rd.
Farmington Hills, MI 48331-3535
Or you can visit our Internet site at http://www.gale.com

LIBRARY OF CONGRESS CATALOGING-IN-PUBLICATION DATA

Does the world hate the United States? / Andrea C. Nakaya, book editor.
    p. cm. — (At issue)
Includes bibliographical references and index.
ISBN 0-7377-2368-8 (lib. : alk. paper) — ISBN 0-7377-2369-6 (pbk. : alk. paper)
    1. September 11 terrorist attacks, 2001—Public opinion. 2. Terrorism—United States—Public opinion. 3. United States—Foreign relations—Public opinion. 4. International relations—Public opinion. 5. United States—Civilization. 6. Anti-Americanism. I. Nakaya, Andrea C., 1976– . II. At issue (San Diego, Calif.)
HV6432.7.D64 2005
973.931—dc22   2004047440

Contents

Introduction

On September 11, 2001, terrorists hijacked four passenger planes and flew two of them into the World Trade Center towers in New York City and one into the Pentagon. The fourth crashed in a field in Pennsylvania. Horrified Americans watched their television sets as people leapt to their deaths from the burning towers and thousands were crushed to death or suffocated under the ruins as the towers collapsed. They saw the enormous hole in the Pentagon smolder and viewed the bodies that littered the Pennsylvania field. Following these terrible images was shock at the realization that someone hated America enough to carry out such devastating attacks.

The September 11 terrorist attacks were the most devastating ever to occur in the United States, and they took many people by surprise. But as international reactions following the attacks revealed, anti-Americanism is not a new phenomenon. It already spanned the globe long before September 11, 2001. While after the attacks, anti-Americanism was slow to reveal itself in most countries, hatred for the United States was immediately and emphatically expressed throughout the Middle East.

Many Arab and Muslim people have long harbored great hatred and resentment for the United States. A major cause of that hatred is American involvement in the Arab-Israeli conflict, which centers on a disagreement between Arabs and Israelis over Israel's right to exist and the Israelis' treatment of Palestinian refugees. The majority of Arabs believe that America's support for Israel—which includes financial and military aid—is hypocritical and harmful to Arabs. They claim, for example, that when Israelis commit terrorist attacks against Palestinians, the United States approves, calling the actions self-defense, while when Palestinians defend themselves, America condemns the actions, calling them terrorist attacks. It is America's support of Israel, they say, that has made the continued oppression of the Palestinians possible.

Arabs' hatred of America became immediately evident when they applauded the September 11 attacks. Osama bin Laden, the terrorist leader believed to be responsible for the attacks, stated: "What America has experienced is God's just pun-ishment for the sufferings they have inflicted on the world of Islam." He was not the only one to celebrate while Americans mourned the carnage in New York, however. Iraqi state televi-sion called the attacks the "operation of the century," deserved by the United States because of its "crimes against humanity." In Palestinian refugee camps across the Middle East, militants fired guns and cheered in celebration.

In the majority of countries around the world, however, anti-Americanism was not the first response to September 11; instead, any existing dislike of the superpower was temporarily overcome by compassion. Indeed, initially, most nations ex-pressed deep sympathy for America's tragedy. In the September 16, 2001, British *Sunday Telegraph*, an American in London re-counted the compassion he received following the attack. He reported:

> Cut off from America, I was nevertheless sur-rounded by goodwill. A saleswoman, hearing an American accent, asked quietly if I'd managed to talk to my parents. A Pakistani driver, teary-eyed, offered his condolences. An American friend told me he had received a sympathy card from his downstairs neighbors, who he barely knows.

Around the world, there were expressions of solidarity with America. In countries such as Australia, Japan, and Russia, people showed their sympathy by placing flowers outside U.S. consulates and embassies. Government buildings in Turkey lowered their flags to half-mast. In the streets of India, Hindus burned an effigy of Bin Laden in protest of the terrorists' ac-tions. Many people emphasized their commonality with Amer-icans. For example, German chancellor Gerhard Schroeder said, "They were not only attacks on the people in the United States, our friends in America, but also against the entire civi-lized world, against our own freedom, against our own values, values which we share with the American people."

However, despite their initial expressions of support for America, even these sympathetic nations had a long, underly-ing history of anti-Americanism. One of the major reasons for this resentment is American foreign policy. Other nations have accused America of being too aggressive, and of pursuing and protecting its own interests at the expense of other nations. Au-thor Muqtedar Khan argues that America's foreign policy has created hatred. He writes: "[America's] exclusively self-regarding outlook, its arrogant unilateralism, its unwise and untrustworthy rhetoric and its belligerent posture, is alienating and angering people in the East and the West." Khan echoes the belief held by many people around the world that the United States "wish[es] to reshape the world to perpetuate America's imperial aspirations. Unfortunately for them the world is unwilling to cooperate. The harder they push the more resentment they will generate."

In addition to its foreign policy, America's culture, which has spread around the world, has elicited both jealousy and disapproval from many nations. One element of that culture is America's way of life, which is often seen as wasteful and harmful to the environment. For example, statistics show that only 4 percent of the world's population lives within the United States, yet America creates 25 percent of the world's carbon-dioxide emissions. Popular culture—music, films, books, advertising, Web sites, and television—is America's most visible and most pervasive export. Many people disapprove of the way of life portrayed in these products and fear the growing Americanization of the world. Writer James W. Caeser describes the strong dislike of U.S. culture that is found globally:

> Anti-Americanism . . . is certainly nothing new. Over a half-century ago, the novelist Henry de Montherlant put the following statement in the mouth of one of his characters (a journalist): "One nation that manages to lower intelligence, morality, human quality on nearly all the surface of the earth, such a thing has never been seen before in the existence of the planet. I accuse the United States of being in a permanent state of crime against humankind." America, from this point of view, is a symbol for all that is grotesque, obscene, monstrous, stultifying, stunted, leveling, deadening, deracinating, deforming, and rootless.

American journalist Charles Krauthammer recognizes the way that even nations who strive to emulate American culture may hate it at the same time. Writing in *Time* magazine, he contends that "envy for America, resentment of our power, hatred of our success has been a staple for decades."

For as long as America has existed, there have been many people around the world who have disliked it for a variety of reasons, including its culture and its actions toward other nations. The September 11 attacks did not change that. Much of the initial outpouring of sympathy quickly evaporated to reveal this negative view of America. Soon there were accusations that America had deserved or even caused the attacks. Many people believed that through its aggressive foreign policy and its negative cultural influence on other countries, America had caused international hatred, which inevitably resulted in the terrorist attacks. Author Todd Gitlin agrees that sympathy for America's loss was quickly replaced by accusations that it was partly to blame for the disaster. He writes:

> As shock and solidarity overflowed on September 11, it seemed for a moment that political differences had melted in the inferno of Lower Manhattan. Plain human sympathy abounded amid a common sense of grief and emergency. Soon enough, however, old reflexes and tones cropped up here and there on the left, both abroad and at home—smugness, acrimony, . . . accompanied by the notion that the attacks were, well, not a just dessert, exactly, but . . . [a] damnable yet understandable payback . . . rooted in America's own crimes of commission and omission . . . reaping what empire had sown.

American writer Harry Browne echoes this opinion. He argues that by its continued violent actions against other countries, America was doomed to eventually see violence against itself. He states: "[America's] foreign policy has been insane for decades. It was only a matter of time until Americans would have to suffer personally for it. . . . When will we learn that we can't allow our politicians to bully the world without someone bullying back eventually?"

The topic of anti-Americanism has been a source of widespread debate for years despite the fact that a large number of Americans often seemed unaware of it. As a result of the September 11, 2001, terrorist attacks, many Americans became acutely aware of the world's hatred for their country for the first time. The authors in *At Issue: Does the World Hate the United States?* offer various perspectives on the extent of anti-Americanism around the world. They also examine the causes of both love and hatred toward the United States, and the implications of these views for Americans.

1

Overview: How the World Views the United States

Pew Research Center for the People and the Press

The Pew Research Center for the People and the Press is an independent opinion research group that studies attitudes toward the press, politics, and public policy issues.

While many people around the world hold positive views of the United States, negative opinions of America are also widespread and are increasing. The majority of countries believe that the United States disregards the views of others in carrying out its foreign policy, and many feel that its policies increase the gap between rich and poor countries. While there is widespread admiration of U.S. technology and of American pop culture, many people dislike the diffusion of American ideas and culture into their society. In contrast to these negative global attitudes, most Americans believe their country's actions and the diffusion of its culture is beneficial to the rest of the world.

Editor's Note: The following viewpoint is excerpted from a 2002 report compiled by the Pew Research Center and is based on data from the Pew Global Attitudes *survey, where face-to-face interviews were conducted with more than thirty-eight thousand people in more than forty-four nations.*

D espite an initial outpouring of public sympathy for America following the September 11, 2001, terrorist attacks, dis-

Pew Research Center for the People and the Press, "What the World Thinks in 2002," *The Pew Global Attitudes Project*, December 4, 2002. Copyright © 2002 by the Pew Research Center. Reproduced by permission.

13

content with the United States has grown around the world [since 2000]. Images of the U.S. have been tarnished in all types of nations: among longtime NATO [North Atlantic Treaty Organization] allies, in developing countries, in Eastern Europe and, most dramatically, in Muslim societies.

Since 2000, favorability ratings for the U.S. have fallen in 19 of the 27 countries where trend benchmarks are available. While criticism of America is on the rise, however, a reserve of goodwill toward the United States still remains. The *Pew Global Attitudes* survey finds that the U.S. and its citizens continue to be rated positively by majorities in 35 of the 42 countries in which the question was asked.[1] True dislike, if not hatred, of America is concentrated in the Muslim nations of the Middle East and in Central Asia, today's areas of greatest conflict.

Opinions about the U.S., however, are complicated and contradictory. People around the world embrace things American and, at the same time, decry U.S. influence on their societies. . . .

Global publics view the United States

The United States and its people are looked upon favorably by much of the world, despite substantial concern over U.S. international policies, its business practices and even its ideas about democracy. The United States is rated favorably by majorities in 35 of the 42 countries where the question was asked. But the U.S. is viewed only *somewhat* favorably in virtually all of these countries. Moreover, negative opinions of the U.S. have increased in most of the nations where trend benchmarks are available.

Opinion of the U.S. varies greatly around the world. More than eight-in-ten respondents in countries such as Venezuela, Ukraine, Ghana, Uzbekistan and the Philippines have a positive view of the U.S. Negative opinion of the U.S. is most prevalent in the Middle East/Conflict Area,[2] but by no means is it confined to those countries. Roughly half of Argentines look upon the United States unfavorably, as do sizable minorities in countries ranging from the Slovak Republic to South Korea.

America's image among its closest allies remains largely positive, although it has declined over the past two years. At least seven-in-ten in Great Britain, Canada and Italy, and

---

1. These survey questions were not permitted in China, and were not asked in the U.S.   2. The Conflict Area in this survey is defined as Egypt, Pakistan, Jordan, Turkey, Lebanon, and Uzbekistan.

roughly six-in-ten in France and Germany, still retain a favorable opinion of the United States. Yet relatively few people in these countries have strongly positive feelings toward the U.S. and favorable opinion has diminished among three of four major U.S. allies in Western Europe.

The picture is similar in Eastern Europe, where solid majorities look favorably at the United States. But up to four-in-ten in the Slovak Republic dislike the U.S. and in four of the six Eastern European countries surveyed opinion of the U.S. has declined [between 2000 and 2002]. Russia is an exception to this trend. Fully 61% of Russians have a positive opinion of the United States, a substantial increase from 37% two years ago [in 2000].

Middle East: Decidedly negative

Public opinion about the United States in the Middle East/Conflict Area is overwhelmingly negative. Even in countries whose governments have close ties with the United States, such as Jordan, Turkey and Pakistan, substantial majorities have an unfavorable view of the United States.

Fully three-quarters of respondents in Jordan, the fourth largest recipient of U.S. assistance, have a poor image of the United States. In Pakistan and Egypt nearly as many (69%) have an unfavorable view and no more than one-in-ten in either country have positive feelings toward the U.S. In Jordan, Pakistan and Egypt, the intensity of this dislike is strong—more than 50% in each country have a *very* unfavorable view.

> *People around the world embrace things American and, at the same time, decry U.S. influence on their societies.*

Public perceptions of the United States in Turkey, a NATO ally, have declined sharply in the last few years. In 1999, a slim majority of Turks felt favorably toward the U.S., but now [in 2002] just three-in-ten do. As is the case in Pakistan, Jordan and Egypt, the intensity of negative opinion is strong: 42% of Turks have a very unfavorable view of the U.S. The same pattern is evident in Lebanon, where 59% have a poor opinion of the U.S.

Uzbekistan, a new U.S. ally in the fight against terror, is a notable exception to this negative trend. By nearly eight-to-one (85%–11%) Uzbeks have a positive opinion of the United States and more than a third (35%) hold a very favorable view of the U.S.

> *" The United States and its people are looked upon favorably by much of the world, despite substantial concern over U.S. international policies. "*

In Lebanon, Pakistan and Egypt, Muslims are more likely than non-Muslims to have an unfavorable opinion of the U.S. This is not the case in Jordan, where both Muslims and non-Muslims hold very unfavorable views of the U.S. In Uzbekistan, Muslims generally have a more positive opinion of the United States than do non-Muslims.

Mixed views of U.S. elsewhere

On balance, Latin Americans have a positive impression of the United States. This is particularly the case in Venezuela, Honduras and Guatemala, where eight-in-ten have a favorable opinion of the U.S. Solid majorities in Peru, Mexico and Bolivia assess the U.S. in positive terms.

Yet people in Latin America's two largest countries—Brazil and Argentina—have a decidedly mixed view of the U.S. Barely half of Brazilians now hold the United States in good stead, and America's image has declined sharply in Argentina. Just 34% of Argentines voice a favorable opinion of the U.S., down from 50% in 2000. Overall, in seven of the eight Latin American countries surveyed, favorable opinion has declined since 2000.

In Asia, there is strong support for the United States in Japan and the Philippines, both long-time U.S. allies. Yet South Koreans are much more skeptical despite that country's close military and economic ties with the U.S. More than four-in-ten South Koreans (44%) have an unfavorable opinion of the U.S.

Nearly half of respondents in Bangladesh (47%) and more than a third in Indonesia (36%), where opinion has declined over the last two years, express an unfavorable opinion of the U.S. America's image in India is also mixed, with a slim majority of Indians (54%) viewing the U.S. favorably.

Publics in Africa have a generally positive attitude toward the U.S. More than three-in-four in the Ivory Coast, Kenya, Mali, Ghana and Nigeria voice favorable opinions of the U.S., and majorities in the other countries agree. . . .

U.S. goals backed, unilateralism decried

In some ways, the war on terror provides a useful prism for analyzing opinion toward the United States. There is broad support for the U.S. goal of combating terrorism, with the notable exception of those countries in the Middle East/Conflict Area. Yet there is an equally strong global consensus that the United States disregards the views of others in carrying out its foreign policy.

This duality of opinion is evident among the United States' closest allies: By wide margins, respondents in Canada and Western Europe support the U.S. struggle against global terrorism. Fewer than three-in-ten in any of these countries oppose that effort. But with the exception of Germany, majorities in these countries believe the United States fails to take into account the interests of their country when making international policy decisions.

This sentiment is strongest in France, where charges of American dominance are longstanding. Even in Great Britain, perhaps the most reliable U.S. ally in the war on terror, half (52%) say the United States disregards British views in carrying out its foreign policy. Germany is the lone exception in this regard, with a slight majority saying the U.S. makes an effort to take Germany's interests into account.

> **❝** *There is a strong sense among most of the countries surveyed that U.S. policies serve to increase the formidable gap between rich and poor countries.* **❞**

A similar pattern is evident in Eastern Europe, where there is even stronger support for the U.S. fight against terrorism. In Russia, for instance, supporters of the fight against terrorism outnumber opponents by nearly five-to-one (73%–16%). As in Western Europe, people in this region overwhelmingly view the U.S. as unilateralist, with no more than three-in-ten saying the U.S. takes their country's interests into account.

Terror fight rejected in Conflict Area

Publics in the Middle East/Conflict Area share Europeans' concerns about U.S. unilateral actions, but strongly oppose the U.S. struggle against terrorism. The single exception is Uzbekistan, which has by far the most favorable opinion of the United States among these countries.

Jordanians, in particular, are overwhelmingly opposed to the war (85%–13%). Majorities in Egypt, Lebanon and Turkey and a plurality in Pakistan, a key U.S. ally in the region, also oppose the war on terror. In Pakistan, Lebanon and Egypt, Muslims are more likely to oppose the U.S.-led efforts to fight terrorism than non-Muslims.

The prevailing opinion among people in this region is that the United States ignores the interests of their countries. This view is as dominant in Turkey (74%), a NATO ally, as it is in Lebanon (77%). By contrast, the growing U.S. military role in Uzbekistan has apparently improved opinion of the United States in that country: Six-in-ten Uzbeks believe the U.S. takes their interests into account and nine-in-ten favor U.S.-led efforts to fight terrorism.

> *In general, people around the world object to the wide diffusion of American ideas and customs.*

Opinion is divided in Latin America over whether the U.S. acts unilaterally in making foreign policy decisions. Majorities in four of the eight countries surveyed—Guatemala, Honduras, Venezuela and Peru—believe the U.S. takes their interests into account when making policy decisions, and there is strong backing in these four countries for the struggle against terrorism.

But in the other Latin American countries surveyed, the dominant view is that the U.S. does not take into account the interests of others. Support for the war on terror also is considerably lower among these countries. This is particularly the case in Argentina, which has the most negative view of the

United States of any country in the region. Three-quarters of Argentines see the U.S. going it alone in setting its foreign policy and just a quarter support the U.S.-led war on terror, underscoring the intensity of negative sentiment toward the U.S. in this country. . . .

Most see U.S. adding to rich-poor divide

In general, respondents to the global survey are more critical of U.S. policies than they are of U.S. values. In nearly every country surveyed, at least a plurality blames differences their country has with the United States on policy disputes rather than on fundamental differences over values. Again, this is true even in the Middle East/Conflict Area.

More specifically, there is a strong sense among most of the countries surveyed that U.S. policies serve to increase the formidable gap between rich and poor countries. Moreover, sizable minorities feel the United States does too little to help solve the word's problems.

These sentiments are not limited to poor countries or those with unfavorable opinions of the United States. In fact, in Germany, France and Canada, roughly 70% say U.S. policies serve to widen the global economic divide. There is less of a consensus on the U.S. role in solving world problems. Outside of Germany, relatively few say the United States does the right amount in this regard, but they disagree about whether the U.S. does too much or too little. Analysis indicates both sentiments are meant as criticisms of the U.S.

In Eastern Europe, as in Germany, more people believe the United States is doing the right amount to alleviate global problems. Solid majorities of Czechs and Slovaks say this, as do roughly half of Ukrainians and Germans. At the same time, most Eastern Europeans fault the U.S. for contributing to the gap between rich and poor nations.

Perhaps not surprisingly, criticisms of the U.S. role in the world resonate strongly in the Middle East/Conflict Area. Three-in-four Egyptians and roughly two-thirds in Lebanon, Jordan and Turkey are critical of America's role in solving the world's problems.

People in Latin American countries, many of which are struggling economically, are also critical of U.S. policies. A plurality in every country says those policies increase the gap between rich and poor, and in all Latin American countries majorities say the U.S. is not doing the right amount to solve world problems.

This same pattern is evident in the Asian and African countries surveyed. Overall these publics feel the U.S. does not do the right amount to solve world problems and adds to the gap between rich and poor countries. Two countries in Africa are important exceptions. In Nigeria and Kenya more people say U.S. policies lessen the gap between rich and poor countries (64% and 41%, respectively). . . .

"Americanism" rejected

In general, people around the world object to the wide diffusion of American ideas and customs. Even those who are attracted to many aspects of American society, including its democratic ideas and free market traditions, object to the export of American ideas and customs. Yet this broad-brush rejection of "Americanism" obscures the admiration many people have for American culture and particularly U.S. science and technology.

Publics in every European country surveyed except Bulgaria are resentful of the American cultural intrusion in their country. The British have the most favorable view of the spread of American ideas, but even half of British respondents see this as a bad thing. Strong opposition to the spread of American customs and ideas is seen in France and Russia, where the number expressing an unfavorable opinion of the United States is relatively high.

> *In most countries American technology is admired more than American ideas about democracy, ideas about business, or popular culture.*

In the Middle East/Conflict Area, overwhelming majorities in every country except Uzbekistan have a negative impression of the spread of American ideas and customs. Just 2% of Pakistanis and 6% of Egyptians see this trend as a good thing. Even in generally pro-American Uzbekistan, 56% object to the spread of American ideas and customs.

The sentiment also appears throughout Latin America and Asia (with the exception of Japan and the Philippines). In Argentina and Bolivia, two countries in which there is considerable antipathy toward the U.S., more than seven-in-ten resent the spread of Americanism. And in Asia, the two countries that most object to American ideas are the predominately Muslim countries of Indonesia and Bangladesh. . . .

Divides on U.S.-style democracy

U.S.-style democracy gets a mixed review in the other Western democracies surveyed. Less than half in every Western European nation surveyed say they like American ideas about democracy. However the U.S. democratic model is viewed positively in many of the democratizing nations of Africa, Asia and Latin America.

> *Americans generally think the export of their ideas and the actions of their government benefit the world, but people in most other countries disagree.*

Views of American democracy are somewhat better in Eastern Europe. Roughly half in the Slovak Republic, Bulgaria, Poland and Ukraine favor American ideas about democracy, and nearly two-thirds in the Czech Republic hold this view. Russians, however, offer a much more negative assessment. Just three-in-ten say they like American ideas about democracy. . . .

The Middle East/Conflict Area has the greatest antipathy toward American ideas about democracy. Consistent with their largely unfavorable views of the U.S., half or more in Turkey, Pakistan and Jordan say they dislike this foundation of the American political system. Opinion is split in Lebanon, with 49% expressing a preference for U.S.-style democracy.

In Latin America, Asia and Africa, public opinion of American democracy generally mirrors overall attitudes toward the United States. Solid majorities like American ideas about democracy in three of the eight Latin American countries surveyed—Venezuela, Guatemala and Honduras. And half or more dislike American democracy in the three Latin American countries with the lowest favorable opinion of the U.S.—Bolivia, Brazil and Argentina.

Among most Asian countries surveyed, American democracy is viewed more favorably. Majorities or pluralities of publics in Asia say they like American ideas about democracy. India, the largest democracy in the world, is an exception, with just 36% positive toward American ideas about democracy. An equal number in India, which is modeled after the British political system, declined to offer an opinion.

African countries generally hold the most favorable opinions toward American ideas about democracy. Majorities or pluralities in all 10 countries surveyed like American democracy, and support is especially strong in Kenya, Ghana, Nigeria and the Ivory Coast. Support is more tempered in Tanzania, Angola, Mali and South Africa.

U.S. technology and Hollywood admired

People around the world have a mixed reaction to exports of American ideas, but they have no such ambivalence concerning U.S. science and technology. Large majorities around the world admire the U.S. for its technological and scientific advances. Moreover, in most countries American technology is admired more than American ideas about democracy, ideas about business, or popular culture. . . .

A dominant image of "what America is" to the outside world is its music, movies and television. American popular culture is readily available nearly anywhere in the world, and in some countries the market for American cultural products is very strong. At the same time, the invasion of American culture is often a complaint, particularly when it is seen as coming at the expense of indigenous cultures.

Still, publics around the world generally embrace American music, movies and television. American popular culture is particularly favored by the young. In nearly every country, the percent of young people who like American movies, music and TV is dramatically higher than among older people. . . .

Opinion of U.S. linked to views of policies

In general, antipathy toward the U.S. is shaped more by what it *does* in the international arena than by what it *stands for* politically and economically. In particular, the U.S.'s perceived unilateral approach to international problems and the U.S. war on terror play large roles in shaping opinion toward the U.S.

Those who think the U.S. does not take their country's interests into account when making international policy and those who oppose the U.S.-led war on terror are much more likely than others to have an unfavorable opinion of the U.S. This is particularly true in the Middle East/Conflict Area, Eastern Europe and Latin America.

Other attitudes are less closely linked with overall opinion of the United States. European and Asian publics that dislike American ideas about democracy are more likely to express an unfavorable opinion of the U.S., and vice versa. In Latin America, by contrast, attitudes toward American technology and scientific advances bear a strong relationship to opinion of the United States. And in Africa, attitudes toward American business practices affect overall opinion of the U.S.

U.S. opinion at odds with global attitudes

There is a great divide between global attitudes and public opinion in the United States. Americans generally think the export of their ideas and the actions of their government benefit the world, but people in most other countries disagree. Those in other countries dislike the spread of American influence and often say the U.S. creates more problems than it solves. These widely different views illustrate the gap between the American public and others, and may help explain why Americans are often surprised by global reactions to the U.S.

2

There Is Widespread Anti-Americanism in Europe

Jean-François Revel

Jean-François Revel, who lives in Paris, is the author of Anti-Americanism.

The majority of Europeans hold a negative view of the United States, which is spread primarily by intellectuals and politicians in Europe. While there was a brief period of European sympathy following the September 11, 2001, terrorist attacks on America, Europe later blamed the attacks on America's foreign policy and condemned the subsequent war on terrorism. American society is widely criticized as inferior to European society; its crime levels are exaggerated and its democratic capitalistic system feared. Many Europeans also resent the position the United States holds as a global superpower, and they scapegoat America to avoid dealing with their countries' problems. This constant criticism of the United States has resulted in an American tendency to disregard all European opinion, even when it is valid.

What picture of American society is likely to be imprinted on the consciousness of average Europeans? Given what they read or hear every day from intellectuals and politicians, they can hardly have any choice in the unpleasant particulars, especially if they happen to be French. The picture repeatedly sketched for them is as follows:

American society is entirely ruled by money. No other

value, whether familial, moral, religious, civic, cultural, professional, or ethical has any potency in itself. Everything in America is a commodity, regarded and used exclusively for its material value. A person is judged solely by the worth of his bank account. Every U.S. President has been in the pockets of the oil companies, the military-industrial complex, the agricultural lobby, or the financial manipulators of Wall Street. America is the "jungle" par excellence of out-of-control, "savage" capitalism, where the rich are always becoming richer and fewer, while the poor are becoming poorer and more numerous. Poverty is the dominant social reality in America. Hordes of famished indigents are everywhere, while luxurious chauffeured limousines with darkened windows glide through the urban wilderness.

Poverty and inequality like this should cause Europeans to cringe in horror, especially since (we have it on good authority) there is no safety net in America, no unemployment benefits, no retirement, no assistance for the destitute—not the slightest bit of social solidarity. In the U.S. "only the most fortunate have the right to medical care and to grow old with dignity," as one writer recently put it in *Libération*. University courses are reserved only for those who can pay, which partly explains the "low level of education" in the benighted USA. Europeans firmly believe these sorts of caricatures—because they are repeated every day by the elites.

> *Criticisms of the U.S. system of law bounce back and forth between the idea that it is paralyzed by legalism and the claim that the nation is a lawless jungle.*

Another distinctive feature of the United States: the pandemic violence. Everywhere you go, violence reigns, with uniquely high levels of delinquency and criminality and a feverish state of near-open revolt in the ghettos. This last is the inevitable result of the deep-rooted racism of American society, which sets ethnic "communities" against one another, and ethnic minorities as a whole against the oppressive white majority. And the unpardonable cowardice and venality that has prevented American leaders from banning the sale of firearms results in regular bloodbaths in which teenagers mercilessly gun down their teachers and fellow students in the classroom. Criticisms of the U.S. system of law bounce back and forth between the idea that it is paralyzed by legalism and the claim that the nation is a lawless jungle.

Yet another universally held conviction is that these social ills are unlikely to ever be cured since Americans make it a point of honor to elect only mental defectives as Presidents. From the Missouri tie salesman Harry Truman to the Texas cretin George W. Bush, not to mention the peanut farmer Jimmy Carter and the B-movie actor Ronald Reagan, the White House offers us a gallery of nincompoops. Only John F. Kennedy, in the eyes of the French, rose a little above this undistinguished bunch, probably because he had the merit of having married someone of French extraction; naturally, this union could not fail to raise President Kennedy's intelligence to at least average level—but doubtless still too high for his fellow citizens, who never forgave him and ended up assassinating him. . . .

Criticism of American society

Many Europeans sneer that America, a society still in a primitive state, ruled by violence and criminality, couldn't possibly have a mature culture. American literature and cinema is said to be an arid desert, devoid of original talent or great creators. They apparently never heard of [authors Edgar Allan] Poe, [Herman] Melville, [Nathaniel] Hawthorne, Henry James, [William] Faulkner, Tennessee Williams, or Scott Fitzgerald. Piercing analysts like Theodore Dreiser, Upton Sinclair, Sinclair Lewis, Frank Norris, John Steinbeck, John Dos Passos, and Tom Wolfe are conveniently ignored. And never mind that American film and television are far more willing to confront sensitive social or political issues than are European productions.

On the whole, American society is sweepingly condemned as practically the worst association of human beings in history. Fresh evidence can do nothing to dispel such views, which, filled with distortion as they are, reflect little on the true strengths and failures of American society. But they tell us a great deal about the psychological problems of those Europeans who proffer the criticisms.

I watched the United States from France and Italy during the 1950s and '60s, and formed my opinion about it through the filter of the European press—which means my opinion was unfavorable. Europeans at this time saw America as the land of McCarthyism and the execution of the Rosenbergs[1] (who we then believed innocent), of racism and the Korean War, and a stranglehold on Europe itself. Then Vietnam became the principal reason to hate America. Even during this period when Europeans completely relied on the United States to protect them against Soviet imperialism, anti-Americanism was almost as virulent as it is today.

For European leftists and the majority of intellectuals—who were likely to adhere to communist ideas—anti-Americanism was rational. This crowd identified America with capitalism, and capitalism with evil. What was less rational was their wholesale swallowing of the most flagrant and stupid lies about American society and foreign policy, with a concomitant flight from accurate knowledge of the political systems that the U.S. was battling.

Reactions to September 11, 2001

A third of a century later, we witnessed something similar. After the terrorist attacks of September 11, 2001, the vast majority of French people expressed sympathy with the U.S. But there were plenty who didn't. On September 16, delegates from the Confédération Générale du Travail, the communist trade union, booed a speaker who called for three minutes of silence in memory of the murdered Americans. Followers of [French politician] Jean-Marie Le Pen on Europe's extreme right celebrated with champagne in offices of the National Front as they watched televised images of the Twin Towers collapsing. So gathered together under the banner of anti-Americanism were all manner of ideological partisans.

A nadir of intellectual incoherence was achieved. After the first gushings of emotion and crocodile condolences, the murderous assaults were depicted as a justified retaliation for evil done by the United States. It's not so surprising that this was a reaction in many Third World countries. Here we see the habitual escape hatch of societies suffering from chronic failure, societies that have completely messed up their evolution toward democracy and economic growth: Instead of looking to

---

1. McCarthyism was a period of intense anticommunism in the United States. American Communists Ethel and Julius Rosenberg were accused of spying for the Soviet Union, and were executed in 1953.

their own incompetence and corruption as the cause, they finger the West in general and the United States in particular. And, after a discreet pause of a few days, claims of American culpability also surfaced in Europe in the press, among intellectuals, and among politicians of the Left and the Right—in France above all.

> *Many Europeans sneer that America, a society still in a primitive state, ruled by violence and criminality, couldn't possibly have a mature culture.*

Declarations multiplied demanding that the U.S. not launch a war against terrorism. A gang of suicidal fanatics, indoctrinated, trained, and financed by a powerful and rich multinational terrorist organization, had murdered more than 3,000 Americans, yet it was the victim who was almost immediately called the aggressor. Shouldn't we ask about the "root causes" that had pushed the terrorists toward their destructive acts? Wasn't the United States in part responsible for what had happened?

Obsessed by their hatred, and floundering in illogicality, Europe's anti-American dupes completely forget that when the U.S. acts against terrorists in her own self-interest, she is also acting in the interest of Europeans, and in the interest of many other countries threatened, or already subverted, by terrorism.

Today's anti-American disinformation is not the result of pardonable, correctable mistakes, but of a profound psychological need to make the U.S. the villain responsible for others' failures.

Exaggeration of American crime levels

Take crime, a subject Europeans love to whip the United States over, while closing their eyes to their own rapidly rising crime levels. The fact is that during the final 15 years of the twentieth century, crime diminished dramatically in the United States. In New York City [former mayor] Rudolph Giuliani cut crime by half in five years. In Europe, disorder has skyrocketed. In France, crime and delinquency *doubled* between 1985 and

1998, and has galloped ahead even faster since then.

Giuliani was mocked in certain French newspapers as "Giussolini." But after having refused for decades to even recognize the existence of a crime problem in their country, French Leftists have finally confessed their "naïve optimism" and leniency toward antisocial behavior. To finally acknowledge 20 years of error is impressive. Yet the minister of justice, Marylise Lebranchu, insisted on doing so with the haughty proclamation that, nonetheless, "The government has no desire to copy the American model." One has one's pride and one's scruples, after all. Overwhelmed by their failure to combat the steadily climbing disorder, and unable to hide from the obvious forever, French authorities in 2001 were forced to sheepishly adopt many American methods of crime fighting. Here and elsewhere, anti-Americanism simply served to cover government incompetence, ideological backwardness, and social disorder.

Criticism of democratic capitalism

For skeptics of democratic capitalism, the United States is, quite simply, the enemy. For many years, and still today, a principal function of anti-Americanism has been to discredit the nation that stands as the supreme alternative to socialism. More recently, Islamists, anti-modern Greens, and others have taken to pillorying the U.S. for the same reason. To travesty the United States as a repressive, unjust, racist society is a way of proclaiming: Look what happens when modern democratic capitalism is implemented!

This is the message of critics not only in Europe, but also in the United States itself, where anti-Americanism continues to prosper among university, journalistic, and literary elites. But in Europe, these ideological reasons for blaming America first are multiplied by simple jealousy of American power. The current American "hyperpower" is the direct consequence of European powerlessness, both past and present. The United States fills a void caused by our inadequacies in capability, thinking, and will to act. . . .

Scapegoating the United States

The fundamental role of anti-Americanism in Europe in general, and particularly among those on the Left, is to absolve themselves of their own moral failings and intellectual errors by heaping them onto the monster scapegoat, the United States of America. For stupidity and bloodshed to vanish from Europe, the U.S. must be identified as the singular threat to democracy (contrary to every lesson of actual history). Thus, during the Cold War, it was dogma among Europeans from Sweden to Sicily, from Athens to Paris, that the "imperialistic" power was America, even though it was the [former] USSR [Union of Soviet Socialist Republics] that annexed Eastern Europe, made satellites out of several African countries, and invaded Afghanistan, even though it was the People's Republic of China that marched into Tibet, attacked South Korea, and subjugated three Indochinese countries. A similar dynamic applies today in the war on terror.

One example of how little credit the U.S. is allowed by the rest of the world is the way the belief spread, and was quickly accepted as fact, that the United States was bent on imposing censorship after September 11 [2001].

The Qatar-based television network Al-Jazeera, and subsequently CNN, had aired a statement by [terrorist] Osama bin Laden in which he gloated over the thousands killed and called for further massacres. According to both American and French terror experts, the tirade may have contained coded messages to "sleepers" in the United States or in Europe relating to projected terrorist attacks. It seemed prudent for the U.S. administration and Congress to appeal to television and radio managers not to broadcast such communiqués.

> **❝**On the whole, American society is sweepingly condemned as practically the worst association of human beings in history.**❞**

Such steps ought to have been understood as legitimate cautionary measures. Instead, a chorus of imprecations was raised around the world. America had imposed censorship, suppressed freedom of the press, violated the First Amendment. The feverish [French newspaper] *Le Monde* headline "Propaganda Rages in the American Media" (October 3, 2001) was typical.

The legions of Muslims living in countries that have never known democracy or the slightest whiff of media freedom apparently felt well qualified to defend these liberties against the only country on the planet where they have never been suppressed. As for the French, they have evidently already forgotten how radio and television were subject to vigilant censorship by the state during the Algerian War [1954–1962], and that scarcely a week went by without a police raid on some newspaper office or other to seize printed material that might "undermine the army's morale."

Protests against America's anti-terrorist policies

Other measures adopted after September 11 to thwart terrorist attacks (similar to those taken in Europe, by the way) raised protests on both sides of the Atlantic. Surveillance of suspects, access to e-mail and bank accounts, giving police the right to open car trunks—were denounced as "totalitarian" by the French League of Human Rights, as well as American civil liberties organizations. Of course, the measures were designed precisely to protect democracy from its totalitarian enemies.

> *For skeptics of democratic capitalism, the United States is, quite simply, the enemy.*

After the 1998 terrorist attacks on U.S. embassies in Africa, Congress set up a National Commission on Terrorism (NCT) to redefine anti-terrorist policy. The commission's report emphasized that "the threat of attacks causing massive loss of human life within our borders continues to grow." On the report's cover was a photo of the Twin Towers, as if by premonition. Predictably, a swarm of leagues, associations, and organizations leapt to block any countermeasures on the grounds that they would "mortally endanger" civil liberties. A group representing Arab-Americans bewailed a "return to the darkest days of McCarthyism." The civil rights chief in the Clinton administration deplored that Americans of Arab origin were unjustly fingered by the commission—though there is not a single mention of Arab-Americans in the NCT report. The resistance was so noisy that the bill which would have mandated certain security measures was effectively buried, never to become law—with results we all know.

The fact that defenders of human rights and liberty wouldn't take into account the right to national defense meant that sensible, foresighted warnings were dismissed as the racist ravings of hawkish fanatics. How did this ingenious propensity for suicide entitle Europeans to brandish slogans denouncing a supposed evaporation of American liberties? Why is the USA casually accused of "fascism," when it is a land that has never known a dictator over the course of two centuries, while Europe has been busy making troops of them? . . .

Resentment of the United States

The real cause of September 11 unquestionably lies in the resentment against the United States, which grew apace after the collapse of the USSR, and America's emergence as the "sole global superpower." This resentment is particularly marked in the Islamic lands, where the existence of Israel, which is blamed on America, is an important motivator. But the resentment is also more quietly present over the entire planet. In some European capitals, the sense of grievance has been raised to the status of an *idée fixe* [a fixed idea], virtually the guiding principle of foreign policy. Thus the U.S. is charged with all the evils, real or imagined, that afflict humanity, from the falling price of beef in France to AIDS in Africa and global warming everywhere. The result is a widespread refusal to accept responsibility for one's own actions.

As for the American "hyperpower" that causes Europeans so many sleepless nights, they should look to their own history and ask how far they themselves are responsible for that predominance. For it was they who made the twentieth century into the grimmest in history. It was they who brought about the two apocalypses of the World Wars and invented the two most absurd and criminal political regimes ever inflicted on the human race. If Western Europe in 1945 and Eastern Europe in 1990 were ruined, whose fault was it? American "unilateralism" is the consequence—not the cause—of the diminished power of the other nations. Yet it has become habitual to turn the situation around and constantly indict the United States. Is it surprising when such an atmosphere of accumulated hate ends in pushing fanatics to compensate for their failures by engaging in carnage?

The refrain of German Greens, French organizations like ATTAC [Association for the Taxation of Financial Transactions for the Aid of Citizens], magazines like *Politis*, Latin American intellectuals, and African editorial writers is that anti-American terrorism can be explained—indeed justified—on the grounds of the "growing poverty" caused by global capitalism, whose forces are orchestrated by the United States. The radical Left in the United States has also made this its rallying cry. The Italian Nobel laureate and novelist Dario Fo, a literary non-entity, put it bluntly: "What are 20,000 deaths [*sic*] in New York compared with the millions caused every year by the big speculators?"

Of course, the Muslim world includes countries that are among the wealthiest on the planet (especially Saudi Arabia, which finances al-Qaeda and other Islamist organizations). Islamic terrorism is the offspring of religious fanaticism; it has nothing to do with poverty; and it cannot possibly lead to any improvement in the lot of backward societies. Islamists utterly reject all measures that might contribute to improvement: democracy, pluralism, intellectual freedom and critical thought, equality for women, and openness to other cultures.

In the two months after 9/11, the phobias and fallacies of traditional anti-Americanism massively intensified. The clumsiest of them was an attempt to justify Islamist terrorism by claiming that America has long been hostile to Islam. The United States' actions historically have been far less damaging to Muslims than those of Britain, France, or Russia. These European powers have conquered Muslim countries, occupied and indeed oppressed them over decades and even centuries. Americans have never colonized a Muslim nation. Americans evince no hostility toward Islam as such today; on the contrary, their interventions in Somalia, Bosnia, and Kosovo, as well as the pressure exerted on the Macedonian government, were designed to defend Muslim minorities. And the U.S.-led coalition that removed the Iraqi army from Kuwait during the first Gulf War acted to defend a small Muslim country against a secular dictator who had used chemical weapons against Muslim Shiites in the south and Muslim Kurds in the north. . . .

European Muslims applaud
the terrorist attacks on America

The day after 9/11, *Le Parisien-Aujourd'hui* published an account of the jubilant atmosphere the previous evening in the eighteenth *arrondissement* of Paris, home to a large Muslim community. "Bin Laden will nail all of you!" was among the more moderate remarks hurled at passersby who didn't appear to be North African. Or: "I'm going to celebrate big time tonight! Those guys were real heroes. That'll teach those American bastards—and all you French are next!" Snippets of this sort were ignored by almost all media.

> *The U.S. is charged with all the evils, real or imagined, that afflict humanity.*

A spokesman for British Muslims named al-Misri likewise called the attacks on the World Trade Center acts of "legitimate self-defense." Another spiritual authority, Omar Bakri Mohammed, launched a *fatwa* commanding the assassination of the president of Pakistan because the latter had sided with [American] President [George W.] Bush against bin Laden. "Islam will Dominate the World" was the slogan on signs held aloft by Islamist demonstrators of British nationality as they marched in October 2001 north of London. Meanwhile, there was not the slightest whisper of protest from all those "moderate" Muslims in Britain or France supposedly opposed to this sort of extremism. The notion that the "immense majority" of Muslims settled in Europe are peacefully inclined must be viewed for what it is: a mirage.

Short-lived European support

Western Europe's antagonism was hardly limited to its Muslim communities. Stunned by the magnitude of the 9/11 crimes and reduced to silence by the wave of solidarity with the U.S., even most long-time America-haters were quiet for a few days. But for a few days only.

The day after 9/11, the editor of *Le Monde*, Jean-Marie Colombani, ran the famous "We Are All Americans" editorial. Hostile reactions to the piece and the headline were numerous and immediate, both among readers of *Le Monde* and on the editorial board. This stemmed from the Left's disinclination, even right after the massacres in New York and Washington, to renounce its demonized image of the United States, an image that it needs all the more since socialism has ended in shipwreck.

Shortly after 9/11 a French spokesman for the activist

group ATTAC quoted the adage: "He who sows the wind shall reap the whirlwind." French prime minister Lionel Jospin seemed to be pointing in this direction when he asked, "What lesson are the Americans going to draw from what has happened?" The lesson, Jospin indicated, should be for the U.S. to moderate her unilateralism. For Cardinal Karl Lehmann, president of the German Bishops' Conference, the lesson to be drawn from terrorism was that "the West must not seek to dominate the rest of the world."

Soon, many European elites insinuated that *jihadist* attacks had some moral justification. These anti-American views began to circulate well before the campaign to dislodge the Taliban[2] kicked off on October 7 [2001]. The bombing which became the most frequently invoked reason to take sides against the U.S. had not yet even begun.

> *// The great irony of this anti-American obsession is that it aggravates the evil that it aims to extirpate. //*

One of the most dishonest objections raised against the campaign in Afghanistan was that Americans had made use of *mujahedin* during the Afghans' war of resistance against the USSR. What was so reprehensible about Ronald Reagan accepting the services of all those willing to oppose the Soviet Union? Was it necessary to wait until all Afghans and Saudis had read Montesquieu and converted to Christianity? Imagine what it would have meant for India, Pakistan, and the Gulf countries— for all of us—if the Soviets had been able to achieve a permanent takeover of Afghanistan. There would have been no [former USSR president Mikhail] Gorbachev, no *glasnost*, and no *perestroika*. Coming from the Europeans, who at the time of the Soviet Afghan invasion quivered with cowardice and debated only if they should or shouldn't participate in the Moscow Olympics, this critique has something, one might say, backward about it.

---

2. the Islamic fundamentalist group that controlled much of Afghanistan from 1996 to 2001

Futility of hating America

Tens of millions of immigrants have streamed into the United States. If the picture of America drawn by the European press is accurate, then those immigrants from all parts of the world were deluded fools. Why choose the American capitalist jungle with all its evils, rather than the lands of peace, plenty, and liberty they came from? Why didn't they write their families and friends basking in the paradises of Ukraine, Calabria, and Greece warning them of the perils of poverty, precariousness, and oppression in America?

The success and originality of American integration stem precisely from the fact that immigrants' descendants can perpetuate their ancestral cultures while thinking of themselves as Americans in the fullest sense, sharing basic ideals across racial and ethnic barriers. In France, the characteristic attitude of newcomers from North Africa, Turkey, and sub-Saharan Africa is predominantly one of alienation, confrontation, rejection, and hatred. . . .

As immigration trends suggest, anti-Americanism is not deeply rooted as a popular prejudice. In Europe, anti-Americanism is much more a hobgoblin of the political, cultural, and religious elites. According to a . . . survey of May 2000, only 10 percent of French feel dislike for the U.S. After September 11, according to another poll, 52 percent of French people interviewed said they had always felt warmly toward the U.S., against 32 percent who said the opposite. Historian Michel Winock concludes that "anti-Americanism is not an attitude of the average French person; it is typical of a certain segment of the elites."

The great irony of this anti-American obsession is that it aggravates the evil that it aims to extirpate, namely the go-it-alone impulse famously ascribed to the U.S. By criticizing the Americans whatever they do, on every occasion—even when they are completely right—Europeans (we are not alone in this, but we lead the dance) compel Americans to disregard our objections—even when *we* are right. The American reflex, conditioned by the constant avalanche of anathemas coming at them, causes them to keep thinking: "They're always blaming us, so why consult them at all? We already know they'll vilify us."

And so America's enemies and allies alike, valuing animosity toward the U.S. over influence on her, condemn themselves to impotence. In the process they strengthen the American superpower.

3

Anti-Americanism Is Not Widespread in Europe

Eric Alterman

Eric Alterman is a columnist for the Nation, *a weekly news-magazine.*

While anti-American sentiments are frequently expressed in Europe, the majority of Europeans do not really hate Americans. Most Europeans are strongly opposed to American policies under President George W. Bush; however, they maintain a good opinion of the American people. While Europeans dislike certain aspects of America, there are also many elements of American culture that they embrace, and this makes it impossible for them to truly hate the United States. After all, there are a large number of similarities between the people of Europe and America, and the good relationship between them is likely to persist, regardless of European disapproval of the U.S. government.

Twenty-four hours or so after landing in Paris for a five-city tour in search of the new European anti-Americanism, I found myself in one of the coolest places on the planet: a big old ugly hockey arena on the outskirts of town, surrounded by 15,000 people waiting for Bruce Springsteen and the E Street Band to come onstage. The concert turned out to be a pretty standard Springsteen concert. But it's always interesting to see him play abroad, and Paris enjoys a special place in Springsteen lore. It was here, back in 1980, that Bruce first talked politics with his fans. Largely self-educated, Springsteen had been given a copy of Allan Nevins and Henry Steele Commager's *A*

Eric Alterman, "USA Oui! Bush Non!: How Europeans See America," *The Nation*, vol. 276, February 10, 2003, p. 11. Copyright © 2003 by The Nation, Inc. Reproduced by permission.

Short History of the United States. He read it and told the crowd that America "held out a promise and it was a promise that gets broken every day in the most violent way. But it's a promise that never, ever dies, and it's always inside of you."

You can tell a lot about a continent by the way it reacts to Bruce Springsteen. Tonight, at the Bercy Stadium, the typically multigenerational, sold-out Springsteen audience could be from Anytown, USA. Everybody knows all the lyrics, even to the new songs. Toward the end of the evening, Bruce announces, in French, "I wrote this song about the Vietnam War. I want to do it for you tonight for peace," and 15,000 Parisians, standing in the historic home of cultural anti-Americanism, scream out at the top of their collective lungs, "I was born in the USA," fists in the air.

You can't be anti-American if you love Bruce Springsteen. You can criticize America. You can march against America's actions in the world. You can take issue with the policies of its unelected, unusually aggressive and unthinking Administration, and you can even get annoyed with its ubiquitous cultural and commercial presence in your life. But you can't be anti-American. [US president] George W. Bush is "like a cartoon stereotype" representing "the worst side of the US culture," Jordi Beleta, 45, told Phil Kuntz of the *Wall Street Journal*, outside Barcelona's Palau Sant Jordi two nights after Paris. "Bruce is real. He's a street man." A Reuters reporter found a similar story in Berlin: "America can keep Bush but Springsteen can come back here as often as he wants," said Rumen Milkov, 36.

> *George W. Bush is 'like a cartoon stereotype' representing 'the worst side of the US culture.'*

To be genuinely anti-American, as the Italian political scientist Robert Toscano points out, is to disapprove of the United States "for what it is, rather than what it does." Bush Administration officials and their supporters in the media would like to confuse this point in order to dismiss or delegitimize widespread concern and anger about the course of US foreign policy. To listen to their words, Europe has become a smoldering caldron of anti-Americanism, in which even our best qualities are held against us by a jealous, frustrated and xenophobic population led by cowardly, pacifistic politicians. The picture painted in the US media is one of almost relentless resentment.

Anti-American sentiments

I heard it first about France, where an anti-McDonald's movement had taken hold, and a xenophobic, neofascist Hitler apologist managed to come in second in a national presidential election. Walk into a French bookstore and you will find titles like *Who Is Killing France?, American Totalitarianism, No Thanks Uncle Sam, A Strange Dictatorship.* French newspapers are filled with blistering criticism of the US role in the world. *Le Monde,* for instance, pulled no punches when it recently termed Bush's Middle East policies "extraordinary, unjust and arrogant."

Well, France is France, but even in Britain, whose prime minister, Tony Blair, has proven Bush's most reliable and articulate ally across the pond, mainstream papers like the *Mirror* announce in large headlines—on July 4, no less—"The USA Is Now the World's Leading Rogue State." (The more liberal *Guardian* said the United States is an "unrepentant outlaw" nation.) Will Hutton, a former editor of the *Observer,* wrote a book portraying the United States as in "the extraordinary grip of Christian fundamentalism"; boasting a "democracy" that is "an offense to democratic ideals," where the "dominant conservatism is very ideological, almost Leninist," and is bolstered by "tenacious endemic racism," with an economy that "rests on an enormous confidence trick," and in which, incidentally, "citizens routinely shoot each other."

I heard it about Italy, where the left was historically dominated by an anti-American Communist Party, and hundreds of thousands gathered to demonstrate against US-led globalization in July 2001 and again against the planned war in Iraq in November [2002].

And I heard it, perhaps most alarmingly, about Germany, which, since World War II, has always been a bastion of support for the United States. In spring 2002, when Bush visited Berlin, the mayor announced that he would have to leave town, and tens of thousands of Germans participated in more than twenty-five large anti-US demonstrations. The sentiment was hardly limited to the demonstrators, moreover. Not only did Chancellor Gerhard Schroeder manage to win re-election by running less against his opponent than against Bush's proposed war in Iraq, refusing cooperation under any circumstances, including full UN [United Nations] approval—but his justice minister, Herta Daubler-Gmelin, even compared Bush to Hitler. (According to *Washington Post* columnist Marc Fisher, Daubler-Gmelin was only saying "what many Germans believe.")

No support for Bush's policies

Meanwhile, beyond the Afghanistan war, I could find no support anywhere in Europe for the Bush Administration's policy priorities: none whatsoever for US withdrawal from the Kyoto Protocol, the Anti-Ballistic Missile (ABM) Treaty or for attempts to weaken the Chemical and Biological Weapons (CBW) conventions, for opposing the Comprehensive Test Ban Treaty and the International Criminal Court (ICC), and not much at all for forcible "regime change" in Iraq. And there was a general disgust with the Bush Administration's formulation—initially explicated in Bush's 2002 State of the Union speech—of an "Axis of Evil" against which all civilized nations must ally themselves. In England, the *Guardian* termed the speech "Hate of the Union." As Jorg Lau, a *Die Zeit* correspondent in Berlin who is quite sympathetic to the United States, ruefully notes, the speech was "unanimously unpopular" in Europe. "I mean it was just so stupid, they are always talking about good and evil, in quasi-religious terms, and it gives us a strange sense of relief. Bush is always showing himself to be utterly stupid. . . . And we just sit back and wait for him to do it. It's unhealthy."

> *Most of what is considered high culture in the United States and much of our popular culture . . . are unthinkable without Europe's . . . influence.*

Even such famously pro-American voices as Chris Patten, the much-admired conservative former governor of Hong Kong—now EU [European Union] Commissioner for External Relations—have taken to complaining about the Bush Administration's launch into "unilateralist overdrive," with its "absolutist" approach to world affairs. These views, moreover, are mirrored almost perfectly by those of Frankfurt University philosopher Jurgen Habermas, the titanic figure of the European democratic (and pro-American) left, who warns, "Many

Americans do not yet realize the extent and the character of the growing rejection of, if not resentment against, the policy of the present American Administration throughout Europe, including in Great Britain. The emotional gap may well become deeper than it has ever been since the end of World War II."

> *Anti-Americanism is a serious concern in many nations on numerous continents. But none of these are in Europe.*

Based on all of the above and far more, a number of American observers have concluded that these European attitudes—which they define as anti-Americanism—are potential grounds for divorce. Indeed, this view is becoming conventional wisdom in the center-right nexus that dominates US mainstream debate. *New York Times* bigfoot pundit Thomas Friedman laments what he terms "the new anti-Americanism, a blend of jealousy and resentment of America's overwhelming economic and military power." Karl Zinsmeister, editor of the American Enterprise Institute's [AEI] monthly magazine, attended a meeting of European movers and shakers in Warsaw in April 2002 and discovered only "animus, jealousy, and willful spite" toward the United States. The conservative economist Irwin Stelzer warns that many European nations "are ceasing, or may have already ceased, to be our friends." Today, "much of the psychological drive for Euro-nationalism is provided by anti-Americanism," notes former *National Review* editor John O'Sullivan. Participating in an AEI-sponsored symposium, the Canadian pundit Mark Steyn added, "I find it easier to be optimistic about the futures of Iraq and Pakistan than, say, Holland or Denmark."

A Euro-American divorce?

An imminent Euro-American divorce is also envisioned in a 11,500-word essay titled "Power and Weakness" by the neoconservative foreign policy writer Robert Kagan, which has taken on a kind of talismanic quality in Europe of late. The essay, which appeared in the Hoover Institution's publication, *Policy Review*, has been translated and reprinted and e-mailed all across the Continent, creating something of a rude awakening for many Europeans. "It is time to stop pretending that Europeans and Americans share a common view of the world, or even that they occupy the same world," Kagan writes. "On the all-important question of power—the efficacy of power, the morality of power, the desirability of power—American and European perspectives are diverging. . . . That is why on major strategic and international questions today, Americans are from Mars and Europeans are from Venus: They agree on little and understand one another less and less. . . . When it comes to setting national priorities, determining threats, defining challenges, and fashioning and implementing foreign and defense policies, the United States and Europe have parted ways."

To the degree that Kagan is correct—and many members of the European cultural and intellectual elite fear he might be, particularly regarding the perception of Europe within the once-Atlanticist US foreign-policy establishment—this is big news. Much of the history of the twentieth century can be told through the rubric of the US-European relationship. Two world wars, the cold war, most of what is considered high culture in the United States and much of our popular culture, including our best cinema and works of literature, are unthinkable without Europe's example and influence. Until recently, so too has peace on the Continent been unthinkable without US leadership. Even today, according to [EU representative] Javier Solana, US-European trade remains the largest trade and investment relationship in the world, totaling roughly $500 billion, with an estimated 6 million jobs in the United States and Europe depending on its continued efficacy. If a divorce is genuinely in the offing, then a tectonic shift in the shape of the world will almost certainly be the result.

> **❝** *What most Europeans seem to recognize is that [America] is a big, beautiful and damn complicated country.* **❞**

But is Kagan really right? Yes, if you take the unilateralist/militarist ambitions of the Bush neoconservatives and the red/green post–New Leftist worldview of the Schroeder government as your templates. But there's a great deal more to the state of transatlantic relations than the hostility of George W.

Bush and his supporters toward Gerhard Schroeder.

Make no mistake, anti-Americanism is a serious concern in many nations on numerous continents. But none of these are in Europe. A recent survey by the Pew Global Attitudes Project found anti-US feelings on the rise in nineteen of twenty-seven nations it investigated. Virtually all the hostility, however, is found in Middle Eastern and Central Asian nations.

Of course, while Europe is making impressive, albeit uncertain, strides toward unification on many levels, the very word "Europe" remains a kind of convenient fiction. But even if you allow for nearly the entire spectrum of views, from the nonfascist right to the noncommunist left, you find virtually no support for the tone or the substance of the current Administration's policies. Neither, however, will you find much of anything that might fairly be labeled anti-Americanism.

Similarities between the US and Europe

In September [2002], when dismay over a growing rift between America and Europe was rife, the German Marshall Fund of the United States and the Chicago Council on Foreign Relations published the results of an ambitious transatlantic survey. Americans and the citizens of six European countries (Britain, France, Germany, Italy, the Netherlands and Poland) were asked about Iraq, foreign policy and one another. You'd never know it judging by the policies of their leaders, but the views and priorities of the United States and Continental populations were remarkably similar. Approximately half of both surveyed populations named global warming as a major threat to national security. (Seventy percent of Americans surveyed said the United States should sign the Kyoto Protocol even when a possible negative impact on the domestic economy was cited; and 65 percent supported US participation in the International Criminal Court even when the possibility of trumped-up charges brought against US soldiers was mentioned.) Support to strengthen the UN stood in the high seventies on both sides, and there was majority support for strengthening institutions like the WTO [World Trade Organization] and NATO [North Atlantic Treaty Organization]. Also, the citizens of these European nations think rather well of Americans. They gave America a favorability rating of sixty-four out of a hundred, just six points below that of the EU. And conversely, nearly 80 percent of Americans surveyed supported strong EU leadership in world affairs. . . .

Talk of divorce between Europe and the United States was under way when [the September 11, 2001, terrorist attacks occurred] and served to remind both sides how many things they held in common, compared with the relatively trivial matters—or so it seemed—that tore them apart. The Continent overflowed with spontaneous symbols of what Schroeder called "unconditional solidarity." *Le Monde* ran a banner headline declaring Nous Sommes Tous Americains [We Are All Americans]. Millions held vigils, rallies and prayer services. Fantastic amounts of money were collected. Stars and Stripes hung everywhere. And NATO's invocation of Article 5[1] of its common defense treaty, as Michael Ignatieff notes, "articulated this sense of a common trans-Atlantic identity under attack."

Anti-Bushism, not anti-Americanism

But the Bush Administration's response quickly dissipated virtually all the sympathy the tragedy inspired. As Jacques Rupnik, a former adviser to both French President Jacques Chirac and Czech President Vaclav Havel, puts it, "Americans are fond of saying, 'The world changed on September 11.' But what has changed is America. The extraordinary moral self-righteousness of this Administration is quite surprising and staggering to Europeans."

Even in those nations like Italy and Spain, where the current conservative governments profess to support the US policies in Iraq, the populations do not. Josep Ramoneda Molins, director of Barcelona's Centre de Cultura Contemporania and a columnist for *El Pais*, informs me that opinion polls in that nation continue to demonstrate a 70 percent rate of opposition to Bush's Iraq adventure. Bush, he notes, "has the absolute complicity of the Spanish [prime minister], but the country does not like him."

It should go without saying that such critical views of US political behavior hardly constitute "anti-Americanism." And perhaps I'm a lousy reporter, but aside from the odd bit of graffiti, I couldn't find much evidence of this allegedly new strain of anti-Americanism anywhere. You could even argue that Europeans demonstrate better taste in American culture than Americans do. Everywhere I went—Paris, Madrid, Barcelona, Rome, Berlin—I found a surprising embrace of things American. . . .

---

1. Under Article 5, NATO members consider an attack against one of them as an attack against them all.

A complicated country

What most Europeans seem to recognize is that this is a big, beautiful and damn complicated country. For every George Bush, we have a [black film director] Spike Lee. . . . Globalization—which for the average European has got to be hard to distinguish from Americanization—appears to evoke little resentment from those who have normally been at the forefront of opposition to the encroachment of (vulgar, materialistic) American culture in Europe. On the left-wing fringes, there's some hatred, sometimes expressed in violence against McDonald's—but the ideologues of this movement, like the famous Jose Bove, will tell you that it's really McDonald's they hate, not the nation that happens to have spawned it. *Le Monde*, the traditional home of snooty Euro-superiority, is now publishing a weekly supplement from the *New York Times* in English. Frachon tells me, "You will find America in every section of the paper. America in rock and roll, movies, in our fashion. On TV too, America is there on a daily basis. This is sometimes irritating, but we are also addicted to it. We try to fight the replacement of French with English, but I do not want to miss *The Sopranos*." . . .

There is a pro-American world out there, in Europe in particular but elsewhere as well. It is just waiting for an America it can respect as well as admire. For all the intentional insults this Administration has thrown their way, our European well-wishers have not given up on what's best in us, no matter how often they feel forced to voice their frustration with the leaders our fundamentally flawed political system presents them with. The time has come for the true democrats among us, of every political stripe, to begin the arduous political and intellectual task of constructing a foreign policy that protects and defends our values as well as our people. Fortunately, it is not a task we will have to undertake alone. We remain blessed with friends and allies who, like a good spouse, know our fears and weaknesses better perhaps than even we do.

If we build it, they will come. Just ask Bruce Springsteen.

4

Central and Eastern Europe Are Pro-American

Radek Sikorski

Radek Sikorski is a journalist and former Polish deputy defense minister.

Central and eastern Europeans have historically shown support for the United States and its policies. This trend continued in 2003 with support for America in its war against Iraq to depose Iraqi leader Saddam Hussein. Pro-American sentiments such as this are the result of America's past stance against the former Soviet Union, which oppressed central and eastern Europeans. Solidarity with America is also the result of anger at the way western European countries—which pride themselves on being anti-American—have treated eastern and central Europe. Despite the fact that supporting the United States may jeopardize their chance for inclusion in the European Union, eastern and central Europeans continue to be friends of America.

"What's the easiest way of gaining security and prosperity for our country?" ran the Communist-era joke in Poland. Answer: "Declare war on the United States, and hope that they invade and occupy." Let us hope there is an Arabic version of this joke and that it's being whispered in the coffee houses of Baghdad right now [in 2003]. It certainly helps to explain why the Central and East Europeans have generally expressed solidarity with America in its confrontation with [Iraqi leader] Saddam Hussein.

That solidarity is especially remarkable for being shared not only by veteran anti-Communists but also by their former tormentors. In Poland, for example, the government is headed by Leszek Miller, once a member of the Politburo, now better known as one of eight signatories to the "New Europe" letter published in the *Wall Street Journal* in support of [U.S. president] George W. Bush.[1] Solidarity with America extends well beyond the ruling circles, too. To take just one case: A friend of mine was in Tehran recently, trying to explain to a multinational audience America's reasons for invading Iraq [in 2003]. Amid the barrage of criticism that ensued, only the Ukrainian, Slovak, and Polish participants came to the Americans' rescue. It is also no accident that the first German politician to break publicly with the policy of the [German chancellor Gerhard] Schroeder government was Angela Merkel, leader of the CDU (Christian Democratic Union) and an "ossie"—that is, someone who spent most of her adult life in East Germany.

To some extent, this is counterintuitive. One would expect the people who spent 45 years being fed anti-American propaganda to be more receptive to fresh charges of American imperialism than those who have enjoyed decades of liberty and prosperity under American protection. Indeed, in Russia, according to a recent television poll, 90 percent of the population opposes the [Iraq] war. So why do the Central and East Europeans nevertheless support America, and why has their own skepticism about the war not fed into anti-Americanism? There are a number of reasons.

Reasons for supporting America

To begin with, America is drawing on a store of goodwill accumulated over the years thanks to its moral stance against the Soviet Union. You might say America is reaping the dividends of Radio Free Europe,[2] Fulbright scholarships,[3] and [former U.S.

---

1. In January 2003 the prime ministers of Spain, Portugal, Italy, Britain, Hungary, Poland, and Denmark, and the president of the Czech Republic, wrote a letter expressing European support for the United States.   2. a covert radio station that was broadcast in Europe during the Cold War by America's Central Intelligence Agency   3. Under the Fulbright program, educational grants are made to U.S. citizens and nationals of other countries, enabling them to spend time teaching or studying in each other's universities.

president] Ronald Reagan. Eastern Europeans are more suscep-
tible to the missionary language of [U.S. president] George W.
Bush today because they themselves were once the beneficia-
ries of a pro-democracy crusade. Nothing jars on East European
ears more than talk of the need to preserve "stability" in the
Middle East, because they remember what "stability" meant in
their own countries not so long ago—the stability of a concentration camp.

> *The U.S. has proved that it has enough friends
> in Europe to keep the continent from uniting
> against it.*

Second, East Europeans are particularly sensitive to imperi-
ous treatment of the kind formerly meted out to them by the
Soviets. Jacques Brezhnev [Jacques Chirac]—as the Slav street is
now calling the French president—put his foot in it badly
when he suggested that EU [European Union] candidate countries should have kept quiet on Franco-German opposition to
the United States. In Poland, he reinforced an impression of
French phoniness going back at least to September 1939, when
France failed to act against Hitler in the West even as Poland
fought in the East. The effete bureaucracy of the European
Union contrasts unfavorably with the American-inspired ca-
maraderie of NATO [North Atlantic Treaty Organization].

Third, while West Europeans may complain of America's
"unilateralism," they themselves practice it towards their
poorer cousins in the East. The *Wall Street Journal* letter came in
reaction to a Versailles declaration of opposition to the U.S.
that France and Germany had issued without consulting anybody else. I don't know whether there is an English word to describe two countries' attempt to impose their will on their
neighbors, but I know we need one. For every one time a U.S.
president has said, "Either you are with us or you are with the
terrorists," East European foreign ministers have heard ten
times, "These are the conditions of your EU membership: Take
it or leave it."

Fourth, we have long memories in my part of the world,
and we remember that the Maastricht Treaty [which led to the
creation of the European Union] was adopted in 1991—in the

very week the Soviet Union collapsed—specifically to draw the West European club more tightly together. Yet that treaty contains not one mention of the most momentous geostrategic event of the century. We had, and still have, the impression that our liberation from the bloodiest tyranny in history was viewed essentially as an inconvenience by our richer neighbors. In our heart of hearts, many of us suspect that the West Europeans regard themselves as superior beings just because they had the good luck to spend the Cold War on the side that was liberated by tanks bearing a white, rather than a red, star.[4]

And the West European reaction to our solidarity with America has reinforced that impression. In the progressive salons of Berlin and Paris, we are now being called "the vassals." Vassals of the United States, that is—even though the new democracies expressed their friendship for the United States without being coerced and, in fact, at some political risk to themselves. We are very touched to see such concern for our independence, especially coming from people who never used such crude words as "Soviet satellites" or "captive nations" back when our all-too-real subjugation was being enforced by the Red Army [of the Soviet Union]. . . .

Results of supporting America

The East Europeans could pay dearly for their solidarity with Uncle Sam. Twice, in 1963 and 1967, France has vetoed the accession into the European community of a country (Britain) that she suspected of transatlantic sympathies. And, let's face it, the 30 years since Britain finally did join—and, now, the case of Iraq—have shown that it was, from the French point of view, a justified fear.

Enlargement of the EU will strengthen the voice of countries that do not share anti-American obsessions, and France's voting power will be correspondingly diluted. I would not put it past the French elite to engineer a mechanism to put off enlargement till kingdom come. If that happens, Europe's entire institutional architecture will blow to bits. In the coming months and years, it will be vital for America's credibility and future influence to show that it pays to be the solid ally of a

---

4. At the end of World War II, Europe was liberated from Hitler; however, much of Eastern Europe came under the control of the Communist Soviet Union and did not regain sovereignty until the late 1980s.

U.S. in need. Relocating some military bases to Eastern Europe as a gesture of reassurance is the least that should be done. . . .

American diplomacy over the war may have been clumsy, but it has at least shown one thing: that it is impossible to unite Europe on the basis of the lowest-common-denominator ideology of anti-Americanism. The U.S. has proved that it has enough friends in Europe to keep the continent from uniting against it. If the crisis over Iraq can finally bury the fantasy of splitting the West by building a rival European superpower, even the recent tantrums of France and Germany may well have been worth it.

5

Arab Nations Hate the United States

Abdel Mahdi Abdallah

Abdel Mahdi Abdallah, who holds a PhD in political science, is an expert in Arab politics and has worked at several research centers across the Middle East.

Many Arabs hate the United States because of the economical, political, and military support it has given to Israel, support that has enabled Israel to defeat its Arab neighbors in the past. In addition, U.S. air strikes and sanctions against Arab countries, America's occupation of Iraq, its support for certain undemocratic Arab regimes, its military bases in Arab countries, and its campaign against Islam have created anti-Americanism in the Middle East. In order to end Arab hatred, the United States should change its policies toward the Arab world and help solve the Arab-Israeli conflict.

The sources of Arab anti-American attitudes are complicated and cannot be explained on the basis of one single factor. Rather, there are internal and external reasons for Arab hatred of the United States, which can be divided into four groups:

1. America's support for Israel and its position on the Arab-Israeli conflict.
2. U.S. military attacks and sanctions against some Arab countries and its military bases in the Arab world.
3. U.S. support for some authoritarian Arab regimes, and its

Abdel Mahdi Abdallah, "Causes of Anti-Americanism in the Arab World: A Socio-Political Perspective," *Middle East Review of International Affairs (MERIA)*, vol. 7, no. 4, December 2003. Copyright © 2003 by MERIA. For a free subscription to MERIA, write gloria@idc.ac.il. To see all MERIA publications, visit http://meria.idc.ac.il. To see the work of MERIA's publisher, the Global Research in International Affairs (GLORIA) Center, visit http://gloria.idc.ac.il. Reproduced by permission.

hostile policies toward Islam, and its own citizens of Arab and Muslim origin.
   4. U.S. hypocritical behavior regarding democracy and human rights in the Arab world.

The following will explore the logic behind each of these arguments.

America's support for Israel and its position on the Arab-Israeli conflict

Political Support. During the last fifty years, the United States stood beside Israel in every conflict with the Palestinians and the Arabs. There is a very obvious reason for that, namely, that America considers Israel its closest ally and the only reliable strategic partner in the Middle East. Therefore, America has provided political support for Israel at the UN [United Nations] Security Council, the General Assembly, and other international organizations. American political support for Israel is widely seen as being unfair and at the expense of the Arabs; consequently, this generated and continues to generate hostility against America in the Arab world.

While the U.S. government was always involved in the efforts to solve the Arab-Israeli conflict, its positions (official and otherwise) always differed with the consensus in the Arab world. The United States, for instance, never called Zionism colonialism; and—with the exception of the 1956 Sinai campaign—it never forced an immediate Israeli withdrawal from occupied Arab territories, as the Arab world demanded. Moreover, the U.S. frequently uses its veto power to block most any resolution at the UN Security Council that would condemn what Arabs see as Israel's excessive use of force against the Palestinians.

Jibril Rajub, security advisor for [Palestinian leader] Yasir Arafat, commenting on one U.S. veto of a resolution said it, "provided cover and protection to the Israeli occupation and support for the destruction and killing of the Palestinians." His statement was shown on all Arab television satellite stations and was broadcast together with a horrible scene of eight Palestinians being killed by the Israeli army in October 2003. There is no doubt that the connection between the U.S. vetoes and the Israeli attacks against the Palestinians will continue to generate hostility and terrorism against the United States throughout the Arab world as long as this conflict continues.

Economic Support. Israel is the largest recipient of U.S. aid in the world, receiving just under one-fifth of total U.S. foreign aid. Since 1949, but especially after September 1970, the U.S. has given Israel over $85 billion in aid and grants. U.S. aid is seen as an American effort to strengthen Israel's economy and as helping to fund Israel's occupation of the Palestinian and Arab territories. Israel, critics of the U.S. argue, is one of the richest countries in the area and there are many Arab and African countries that are in need of such aid more than Israel. At the same time, other Arabs argue the opposite: that without this aid Israel's economy would collapse.

It is worth noting here that the United States has provided many Arab countries, including Egypt, Jordan, Morocco, the Palestinian Authority and others with economic aid, however, the people saw that aid as U.S. support for the undemocratic regimes in those countries and not for real development.

> *During the last fifty years, the United States stood beside Israel in every conflict with the Palestinians and the Arabs.*

Military Support. The United States provides Israel with sophisticated arms such as attack helicopters, jetfighters, and missiles that are used to target Palestinians, frequently killing innocent civilians (which most Arabs believe is done intentionally), destroying homes, stores, and other buildings, and were for many years used against Lebanon, as well as against the Iraqi Osiraq reactor in 1981 and Syria in the fall of 2003. The United States is committed to maintaining Israel's security as well as a qualitative edge over all Arab countries, which has enabled Israel to defeat the Arab countries in some of its wars. U.S.-Israel joint arms development and sales is seen as another form of assistance to Israel, which allows it to maintain its military superiority over the Arabs. One commentator explained U.S. military aid as perhaps stemming "from a desire for Israel to continue its strategic and political dominance over the Palestinians and the region as a whole. It has long been in the U.S. interest to maintain a militarily powerful and belligerent Israel dependent upon [itself]. Real peace could undermine such a relationship."

Some Arabs argue that without this generous American military aid, Israel would have been unable to defeat the Arab armies and continue its occupation of Arab land. [Former Egyptian] President [Gamal Abdel] Nasser announced during the 1967 war that the American and the British were involved in attacking Egypt (though later accounts would prove this assertion false) and that they provided Israel with military assistance. The Arab masses, according to [author Adnan] Abu-Odeh, "Believed that the Arab defeat was due to the Americans and British offering military assistance to Israel."

This interpretation of the relationship between U.S. support for Israel and its victories over the Arabs has been accepted and repeated again and again by many Arab politicians, military officers and journalists during the last fifty years. This view was strengthened by repetition in the Arab mass media, including television, radio, newspapers, seminars, rallies, thousands of sermons in mosques, and by the political elite and the regimes themselves. All those resources repeat and emphasize that U.S. support for Israel is unfair, unbalanced, racist, and the main reason for Israel's victories and humiliation of the Arabs. These resources use the Israeli air raids and bombardment of Palestinian and Lebanese territories, the killing of many civilians, and the destruction of their homes and property by U.S.-made jetfighters, helicopters, artillery and tanks to support this view. All of which generates anti-Americanism.

> *The United States provides Israel with sophisticated arms such as attack helicopters, jetfighters, and missiles that are used to target Palestinians.*

The American occupation and similar actions in Iraq undoubtedly contributed to the anti-Americanism and anger among Arab peoples. Arab satellite stations and mass media provide 24 hour coverage of Israeli and American aggressive actions in Palestine and Iraq and commentators passionately make the link between the two cases.

Here as above, it must be mentioned that the United States provides many Arab countries (such as Egypt, Jordan, Morocco and Yemen) with military aid and training, while it provides sophisticated arms training and military protection to others, such as the GCC [Gulf Cooperation Council] countries. But again, such aid is seen as a U.S. effort to strengthen the ability of friendly, yet undemocratic, Arab regimes to stay in power and to suppress their people, rather than to defend Arab countries or to fight Israel.

U.S. Policies Toward the Arab-Israeli Conflict. The Arab perception of the American position is that it is completely supportive of Israel, and that America always adopts Israel's point of view in this conflict. Many Arabs see the U.S. war and occupation of Iraq as part of a U.S. effort to protect Israel as well as to obtain oil for itself.

> *The United States has pursued what were perceived to be hostile and aggressive policies towards many Arab countries.*

On the first count, Arab political figures say that the U.S. administration condemns the killing of Israelis by Palestinians but not the other way around. They add that the United States uses double standards when dealing with the question of nuclear weapons in Israel and the Arab world since the United States has never brought Israel's capabilities to the attention of the UN nor initiated sanctions against Israel for its unconventional weapons programs, though it has done both against Arab states. The Arab public sees U.S. positions in the Arab-Israeli conflict as biased and feels the U.S. government is not an honest broker in the conflict.

The question that the Arabs have continuously asked themselves for the last half-century is why the United States provides Israel with such generous political, economic and military support. The answer that has been given to them is that the West and especially America created Israel and that Israel was their only reliable strategic alliance against the Soviet bloc during the Cold War and is still their outpost in their efforts to control the area.

What is not mentioned is that America is also committed to the security and existence of many Arab regimes and provides them with military and economic aid. But the Arab people don't appreciate U.S. economic and military aid to those countries because they believe that U.S. aid simply supports those undemocratic regimes and not the countries' people. Of course, Arab regimes and Arab media do not discuss U.S. aid to their own countries very much, and this has led many to think that a large part of this aid eventually ends up in the private accounts of corrupt members of the regimes.

U.S. policies and behavior towards some Arab countries

U.S. Attacks and Sanctions Against Some Arab Countries. The United States has pursued what were perceived to be hostile and aggressive policies towards many Arab countries, such as its air strikes against Libya, Sudan and Iraq, which resulted in the deaths of many innocent Arab civilians. This is in addition to its [2003] invasion and occupation of Iraq on false premises, its political and economic sanctions against Iraq, Libya, Syria and Sudan, and its allegedly inhuman treatment of Arab and Muslim prisoners—especially in Camp X-ray, the Guantanamo Bay detention center [after the September 11, 2001, terrorist attacks]. The scene of heavily chained prisoners led and guarded by armed solders with their heads pushed down was portrayed as outrageous and cruel.

This is also in addition to reports of the American government's discrimination against its own Arab and Muslim citizens, especially after the September 11th attacks. Thousands of Arabs and Muslims were reported to have been detained or mistreated due solely to their ethnicity or religion, which was perceived as the result of a racist policy. The Arab media reported that, as a result of this policy, thousands of Arabs quit their studies or work and returned to their countries preaching anti-Americanism. U.S. embassies in the Arab world refused to give visas to many Arab citizens and there was reportedly mistreatment of Arabs at U.S. airports. The United States was also said to be carrying out "media campaigns against Islam."

It is worth noting here that U.S. involvement in the Iraq issue in the 1990s came as a response to a request from Kuwait, Saudi Arabia and other Arab countries, who then invited the U.S. armed forces into their respective countries. Egyptian, Syrian, and GCC units fought under the leadership of U.S. forces in the 1991 war against Iraq [which had invaded Kuwait], and the GCC countries financed a majority of that war. U.S. sanctions against Iraq, it is claimed, were enacted on behalf of the GCC countries in order to weaken the Iraqi regime and to reduce its threat to those countries. In return, the GCC countries provided America with bases and logistical support to fly over Iraq during the 1990s.

U.S. Military Bases in Some Arab Countries. The presence of U.S. military bases in Saudi Arabia, Qatar, the UAE [United Arab Emirates], and Bahrain—as well as regular military training and exercises with Egypt, Jordan and Morocco—is viewed as a new American colonialism and a way to strengthen American control over Arab oil. In addition, this new American colonialism is believed to seek control over Arab political and economic affairs in order to secure American domination of the Middle East. America has used those bases on a number of occasions, such as its invasion of Afghanistan, the ten years it enforced the no-fly zone over Iraq, and later to invade and occupy Iraq. Similarly, one frequent claim is that America supports the ruling regimes in the region, securing their loyalty to America by training troops loyal to the regime and by sharing intelligence.

> *U.S. government officials frequently speak about democracy and human rights, but their actions often do not support either democracy or human rights in the Arab world.*

Rami Khouri, a well-known analyst in the region, stated the suspicion succinctly, "There is a sense by many ordinary people and politicians that the moves against Iraq are an effort to redraw the map for the strategic interests of the United States and Israel." Similar arguments have been made by [terrorist leader] Usama bin Ladin, who said that the existence of U.S. military bases in Saudi Arabia, especially near Mecca, violated Islamic law, which forbids any non-Muslims from entering that sacred area. He called for jihad against the United States stating as his primary reason, "The very presence of the United States occupying the Land of Islam in the holiest of places in the Arabian Peninsula where America is plundering its riches, dictating to its rulers, and humiliating its people."

It is worth noting once again that the U.S. bases and training exercises came in response to requests from some Arab countries and thus do not constitute imperialist actions. Nevertheless, many Arabs argue that the establishment of U.S. bases is intended to provide support and protection for Israel, some friendly Arab regimes, and to secure American interests in those countries.

U.S. Attacks Against Islam and the Clash of Civilization Thesis. In his well-known "clash of civilizations" thesis, Samuel Huntington argues that cultural and religious differences are a major cause of international conflict in the post–Cold War era and asserts that Islam in particular encourages Muslim aggressiveness toward non-Muslim peoples. According to Huntington, "Some Westerners have argued that the West does not have problems with Islam but only with violent Islamic extremists. . . . But evidence to support [this assertion] is lacking. . . . The underlying problem for the West is not Islamic fundamentalism. It is Islam."

Although the administration of [U.S.] President George W. Bush insists that the U.S. war on terrorism is not a war on Islam, this is not what is reported in the Arab media, in speeches by Arab leaders, and in the minds of many Arabs. For example, Bashar al-Asad, the Syrian leader, told the 10th Islamic Summit Conference in Malaysia that the September 2001 attacks on the United States:

> Provided the opportunity and pretext for a group of fanatics and ill-intentioned people [who were part of U.S. administration] to attack human values and principles. . . . Those fanatics revealed their brutal vision of human society and started to market the principle of force instead of dialogue, oppression instead of justice and racism instead of tolerance. They even began to create an ugly illusory enemy which they called 'Islam,' and made it appear as if it is Islam [was responsible] while Islam is completely innocent of it.

Malaysian Prime Minister Mahathir Muhammad went on to say, "We, the whole Muslim umma [community], are treated with contempt and dishonor. Our religion is denigrated. Our holy places desecrated. Our countries are occupied." All Muslims were suffering 'oppression and humiliation' with their religion accused of promoting terrorism.

These ideas are given credence by the statements of some U.S. religious figures, which are widely reported in the Arab media. For example, [evangelist] Rev. Franklin Graham said of Islam, "I believe it's a very evil and wicked religion." Fox News Network talk-show host Bill O'Reilly denounced the teaching of "our enemy's religion" and compared the assignment of a text on Islam in an American university to teaching *Mein Kampf* [by Adolf Hitler] in 1941. After September 11th, many journalists, television presenters, academics, and members of Congress attacked Islam or portrayed Arabs as terrorists.

> *// Arab hostility is primarily directed at specific U.S. policies, not at America or the American people. //*

However, some Western polls concluded, "Islamic attachments have relatively little explanatory power so far as political attitudes are concerned. There is at best a weak relationship between the degree of religious piety or strength of Islamic attachment on the one hand and, on the other, attitudes either about war and peace or about democracy." In other words, those individuals for whom religion is most important are no less likely than others to favor compromise with the United States, democracy, human rights and so forth. In Jordan, over 90 percent of university students believe that there is no contradiction between Islamic teachings and democracy or human rights.

When the United States asks for changes in the Arab media or educational system, some Arabs respond that this is part of [an] . . . effort to dominate the region [by America and Israel]. They see American efforts to modernize Arab curriculums and textbooks as a "deliberate U.S. policy to impose American-Israeli culture on the Arab world and to destroy Arab culture."

U.S. support for some Arab regimes and hypocritical behavior

U.S. Support for Some Authoritarian Arab Regimes. The ways in which U.S. policies are explained to the people might be convenient to some Arab regimes, diverting the anger of the masses onto America instead of toward the many political and economic problems in their countries. The paradox here is why America has never challenged these hostile Arab regimes' positions. Why does the U.S. government continue to support those regimes that advocate anti-Americanism?

The only logical explanation for the U.S. position, it is commonly believed among Arabs, is that the United States believes that the alternative to the present governments would be Islamist regimes. This mistaken support of the status quo increases anti-Americanism by associating the United States with the current rulers. An alternative would be to press the regimes for real and gradual change toward democracy. Fortunately, the U.S. government has begun to realize its mistake and has started to develop a new policy.

But another source of anti-Americanism has been America's support for some authoritarian Arab regimes that are unpopular with their own people. The United States provides those regimes with a large amount of economic and military aid, which helps them stay in power. The United States has never linked its aid to a process of democratization and therefore, this aid was never seen as aid for the people. U.S. economic aid is very much needed in many Arab countries but it should be directed to socio-economic development and not used for security or for buying useless arms and military hardware. [Author] Daoud Kuttab has argued: "When the average Arab citizen tries to reconcile his desire for domestic freedom, his feelings of frustration at home, American support for his government, and the increasing presence of Western culture he is caught in the middle. It is easier to lash out at a distant America than to risk raising one's voice against the local dictators." He added that popular Arabs' support for America "will be hard to muster until Arabs are able to live as they wish, without oppression and without restrictions. Once Arabs are able to voice concerns about their own government without fear of reprisals, their focus will turn inward.". . .

> *Anti-American sentiment in the Arab world has become an important issue in U.S.-Arab relations and a major concern for both sides.*

American Hypocritical Behavior Toward the Arab World. U.S. government officials frequently speak about democracy and human rights, but their actions often do not support either democracy or human rights in the Arab world. Rather, democracy is undermined by the American support for some Arab repressive regimes. Furthermore, the U.S. government never pressed Arab regimes to become democratic nor to respect human rights. Arabs say America would never call for democratization because those undemocratic regimes are the best agents of America's interests. They sell oil at prices said to be determined mainly by America, open their countries for U.S. military bases, facilitate American control and domination over the Arab Worlds' economic resources (including oil), and convert the Arab world into a huge consumer market for U.S. products. In addition, Arab governments are purported to make unnecessary large arms deals worth billions of dollars, which allegedly give them a capacity to suppress the people rather than use the money for socio-economic development.

This hypocritical behavior is said to be reflected in a U.S. invasion of Iraq to "liberate" those people while a regime in Kuwait was reinstalled without the U.S. demanding major democratic reforms, or America defending Saudi Arabia without asking that government to widen political participation to include the masses, or the U.S. not objecting to a military coup in Algeria against the Islamist party after it won the elections. Aside from all this, the dominant view in the Arab world is that U.S. foreign policy regarding the Arab-Israeli conflict is shaped by the pro-Israel lobby.

Arab anti-Americanism as a new phenomenon

A number of recent opinion surveys in Arab and Islamic countries provide a look at the views of ordinary men and women, and at the factors shaping these attitudes and values. Until recently, there has been very little serious political attitude research conducted in the Arab world, which has made it difficult to challenge stereotypes about Arab public opinion. In more recent surveys, however, there emerges a consistent patter of a "strong dislike for American foreign policy but much more nuanced, and often-quite positive, attitudes toward American society and culture and toward the American people." This confirms what Americans visiting the Arabic world often hear in one-on-one conversations, summarized by one researcher as: "When you return to the U.S., give my love to the American people and tell your president to go to hell!"

A Zogby [international research firm] poll conducted in spring 2002 confirms this notion and shows that "men and women in different age groups have favorable opinions about U.S. education, freedom, and democracy [while] almost no re-

spondents have a favorable attitude toward U.S. policy. . . ."
Monem also asserted a similar view:

> Ask anyone in Egypt what country they would like
> to visit, and they will probably say America. Ask
> them what movie they would like to see and it will
> probably be an American film. Ask them what
> school they would like to attend and they will
> name an American university. They may disagree
> violently with American policies, but they don't
> hate America. This is the paradox.

[Scholar] Ussama Makdisi argues that "anti-Americanism is
a recent phenomenon fueled by American foreign policy, not
an epochal confrontation of civilizations. While there are certainly those in both the United States and the Arab world who
believe in a clash of civilizations and who invest politically in
such beliefs, history belies them." Over the course of the twentieth century, and especially after the Cold War, U.S. policies toward the Arab world are said to have changed profoundly.

But Arab hostility is primarily directed at specific U.S. policies, not at America or the American people. Thousands of
Americans work and travel in the Arab world and the majority
of Americans enjoy the experience, have Arab friends, and
rarely suffered personal harm, at least until U.S. direct military
intervention in the region began in the early 1990s. . . .

Anti-American sentiment in the Arab world has become an
important issue in U.S.-Arab relations and a major concern for
both sides. There are however, different views and explanations
regarding the roots and causes of this phenomenon. A key aspect
is the continuing frustration that plagues the majority of the
Arab peoples as a result of the continuation of the status quo;
and this same frustration is undoubtedly a factor in terrorism. . . .

This paper has argued that Arab sentiments are neither
fixed nor static, nor are they irrational. Rather, Arab attitudes
of anti-Americanism are primarily a result of U.S. support to Israel and American hostile policies toward the Arab world, and
if those policies change so will Arab perceptions and attitudes.
It suggests that solving the Arab-Israeli conflict, ending the U.S.
occupation of Iraq, closing its military bases in the Arab world,
ending its military support to some Arab authoritarian regimes
and pressing for democratization in the Arab world would end
anti-Americanism among the Arabs.

6

Many South Koreans Dislike America

Seung-Hwan Kim

Seung-Hwan Kim is a professor of international affairs at Myongji University in Seoul, South Korea.

Anti-Americanism is growing rapidly in South Korea. This anti-American sentiment has been caused by resentment and skepticism of American policies toward Korea, and the presence of U.S. military bases in that country. It is also a result of negative images of the United States presented in the Korean media and Korean nationalism. Anti-Americanism in Korea is unlikely to disappear and could be harmful to both the United States and Korea. It is in the best interests of both countries to take steps to improve the image of the United States in Korea.

Anti-Americanism is growing at a startling rate in South Korea, potentially escalating into a serious problem that could jeopardize the future of the U.S.-Korean alliance. Although previously limited to the concern of a minority of leftist nongovernmental organizations, student activists, and some liberals, anti-American sentiments have now spread into almost all strata of Korean society, ranging from the policy-making elite in the government and the intellectuals to members of the middle class and the younger generation.

Beyond its overall increase, the sources of anti-Americanism have become more complex and diverse. Following the attacks on September 11 [2001], ironically, U.S. policy toward North

Seung-Hwan Kim, "Anti-Americanism in Korea," *Washington Quarterly*, vol. 26, Winter 2002/2003, pp. 109–22. Copyright © 2002 by the Center for Strategic and International Studies and the Massachusetts Institute of Technology. Reproduced by permission of the MIT Press, Cambridge, MA.

Korea has become another cause of popular South Korean resentment toward the United States. According to a [2002] public opinion poll, 63 percent of South Koreans have unfavorable feelings toward the United States, and 56 percent feel that anti-Americanism is growing stronger in the Republic of Korea (ROK). Unless Washington and Seoul work together on a course of action to counter this trend, these popular Korean attitudes could become a critical wildcard harming the future of the U.S.-Korean relationship.

Saber rattling and sunshine

Following [U.S. president] George W. Bush's announcement of a new U.S. policy toward the Korean peninsula in his January 29, 2002, State of the Union address, a new wave of resentment toward the United States hit South Korea. Bush's denunciation of North Korea as part of an "axis of evil" and his threat to take preemptive actions against [North Korean capital city] Pyongyang have angered many in South Korea, leading them to believe that the United States was escalating the possibility of a crisis on the peninsula as part of its global war on terrorism. Many Koreans felt that Bush's new policy put South Korea's security interests at risk and poured ice water on the country's efforts to continue overtures with the North.

U.S. policy toward the North after September 11 and the South's "sunshine policy"[1] engaging the North complicate the U.S.-ROK relationship because of Bush's and ROK president Kim Dae-jung's diametrically opposed views on North Korea. Kim Dae-jung has a positive view of the leadership of the Democratic People's Republic of Korea (DPRK). He believes that the DPRK is changing to ensure the survival of its regime and that South Korea's engagement policy will eventually bear fruit. Washington's hard-line approach toward North Korea attempts to prevent Pyongyang from assisting terrorists and developing weapons of mass destruction (WMD), including missiles, nuclear weapons, and chemical and biochemical weapons. North Korea is presently included on the U.S. Department of State's list of states that sponsor terrorism and has a record of exporting missile technology and military equipment to rogue states, including Iraq, Iran, and Syria. Bush questions the wisdom of

1. South Korea's policy of actively engaging North Korea in an attempt to improve relations between the two countries

negotiating with North Korean leader Kim Jong-il, whom he perceives as a dictator and an unreliable leader who starves his country's people yet earns millions from selling weapons to rogue states. Bush's new policy, however, was a major blow to Kim Dae-jung, who has been pursuing engagement with North Korea since entering office. Bush's harsh rhetoric toward the North and the disastrous U.S.-ROK summit in March 2001[2] gave rise to the widespread perception in Seoul of the Bush administration's disapproval of Kim Dae-jung and his engagement policy.

> *Although previously limited to the concern of a minority . . . anti-American sentiments have now spread into almost all strata of Korean society.*

Consequently, anxiety and resentment among liberal South Korean politicians and some government officials surrounding Kim Dae-jung have erupted. South Korea's ambassador to the United States, Yang Sung-chul, complained that Bush's speech dismayed the Korean government and warned about "unnecessary tensions or escalation of rhetoric." Some liberal Korean legislators issued a statement criticizing the U.S. administration, saying that "Bush and his hawkish foreign policy advisers were heightening tensions on the Korean peninsula and expanding the war on terrorism in an attempt to justify an increased U.S. defense budget, detract from the Enron scandal,[3] and lay the groundwork to win the November [2002] elections." More direct criticism has come from the members of Kim Dae-jung's inner circle. In December 2001, the spokesman of his ruling New Millennium Party remarked that the "U.S. government was thwarting the sunshine policy despite the clear sign from the North to expand cooperation." Immediately after his visit to Pyongyang in April 2002, Kim Dae-jung's confidant and special adviser on North Korean affairs, Lim Dong-won, blamed the Bush administration for the failure of Kim Jong-il's reciprocal visit to Seoul. The South Korean gov-

2. Following the summit, the North called off scheduled talks with the South. Many people believed this was a result of Bush's criticism of the North.   3. The American Enron Corporation had reported false profits, resulting in Enron's bankruptcy in 2001—one of the largest in U.S. history.

ernment had hoped to highlight Kim Dae-jung's engagement policy with the North through such a visit.

The negative attitudes of leading Korean policymakers toward the Bush administration have resonated within the general public. Korean resentment erupted into strong anti-American protests across the country during Bush's visit to Seoul in February 2002. Some student activists intruded and staged violent protests in the U.S. Chamber of Commerce under the slogan "opposition to the visit of President Bush." A large majority of Koreans who have desired reconciliation with the North saw Bush's approach as unilateral and high-handed. Much of the Korean public views the United States as an angry and mighty giant who does not care about its friends. A February 2002 public opinion poll found that 6 out of 10 Koreans are not "sympathetic" to Bush's "axis of evil" statement linking North Korea to Iraq and Iran. . . .

Sources and amplifiers

Believing that Bush's harsh rhetoric after September 11 created the problem, however, would be naïve, when it was merely a spark that inflamed anti-American sentiment in South Korea that already existed, if to a lesser extent, prior to September 11. U.S. military bases on Korean soil, the Korean media's negative image of the United States, changing demographics, Korean nationalism, and skepticism have all contributed to rising resentment toward the United States. The foundation of this trend may be general impressions of U.S. arrogance globally and a sense of U.S. domination in South Korea in particular that have directly fostered resentment, and even humiliation, among the Korean people.

As memories of the Korean War fade and the threat from the North diminishes, long-standing resentment over the basing of 37,000 U.S. troops in South Korea only grows stronger. Issues surrounding U.S. bases, such as noise and environmental pollution, [U.S. base] Yongsan's location in midtown Seoul, and the Status of Forces Agreement, have rankled Korean pride and offended notions of sovereignty. An accident in June 2002, in which two middle-school girls were struck and killed by a U.S.-armored vehicle participating in a training exercise in Uijongbu City, 25 miles north of Seoul, further exacerbated Korean ill will toward the United States.

Although the accident was clearly a mistake, the way it was

mishandled and a sense of U.S. influence in both the investigation and the judicial process caused a flurry of anti-American protests. The United States' insistence soon after the incident that "no one was at fault" was perceived as an extension of U.S. arrogance and even seemed degrading to the Korean people. Furthermore, when Koreans learned that the U.S. Army led the investigation while the Korean police and military had little influence and that U.S. Forces Korea (USFK) flatly declined the Korean request for jurisdiction, many Koreans—from students to policymakers to intellectuals—saw the situation as indicative of the unequal, U.S.-dominated nature of the bilateral relationship in general. They demanded the revision of the Status of Forces Agreement [which defines the legal status of U.S. forces]. As the level of anti-American protests increased, U.S. soldiers unprecedentedly held a candlelight vigil for the accident victims, and U.S. secretary of state Colin Powell and U.S. ambassador Thomas Hubbard officially apologized and expressed regret. Nevertheless, the anger of the Korean public has not subsided.

Negative media portrayals

The negative image of the United States portrayed by the media further exacerbates anti-American sentiment in South Korea. Media reports often ignore the positive aspects of U.S. policy and frequently create a negative climate in which the United States can be criticized. An incident during the 2002 Winter Olympics held in Utah—when Korean short-track skater Kim Dong-sung lost to Apollo Anton Ono, a U.S. contender, as a result of a controversial ruling by an Australian judge—was an example in which the media coverage inflamed resentment toward the United States. Although the United States had no involvement in this incident beyond the venue, the country was blamed. When officials disqualified the Korean skater in the last lap of the final short-track race for blocking the U.S. skater, the Korean public became furious at the U.S. skater for putting on what they believed was an acting performance that eventually won him a gold medal. The Koreans' belief that the U.S. gold medal was stolen was supported by the U.S. broadcasting company NBC's Internet poll conducted in the United States immediately after the incident, to which 96 percent of respondents answered that the ruling was "unfair." The reenactment of the Winter Olympics speed-skating event by Korean soccer players after their first goal against the United States in the 2002 World Cup reflected the extent of Korean displeasure with events in Utah.

Given these circumstances, Korean anger intensified when NBC's "Tonight Show" host Jay Leno made the racially discriminatory remark, as he defended the referee's decision at the Winter Olympics, that "the Korean player had been angry enough to have kicked and eaten a dog when he returned home." South Korea's major television networks repeatedly aired Leno's comments, accompanied by negative comments on U.S. attitudes, while condemnation and protests against the United States flooded the Internet and spread throughout the country. In an unprecedented move, some Koreans even started an anti-American campaign by boycotting U.S. products, including F-15E fighter aircraft and Coca-Cola, as well as franchised U.S. restaurants such as McDonalds.

> *The negative image of the United States portrayed by the media further exacerbates anti-American sentiment in South Korea.*

Korea's changing demographic structure is also a major factor in the rise of anti-Americanism. Members of the generations involved in the Korean War and the Vietnam War, in particular, have an emotional tie to the United States, based on shared Cold War experiences. This generation is aging, however, and constitutes a diminishing percentage—21 percent—of South Korea's population. Two-thirds of the country's population is under the age of 40, and younger Koreans' attitudes toward the United States are knotty. They recognize the importance of the U.S.-ROK alliance for their security against North Korea, but they are reluctant to tolerate perceived U.S. arrogance and U.S. political as well as economic domination. In addition, they have a more negative image of the United States' status as the world's only superpower. Because they tie U.S. political and economic domination to the presence of U.S. forces in South Korea, younger Koreans increasingly want to see a significant reduction of U.S. forces in South Korea or even a complete withdrawal. . . .

Some members of another sector within the Korean general

population—intellectuals—consider the United States an arrogant, unilateralist nation that disregards South Korea and its national pride. Despite all the emphasis on the importance of the U.S.-Korean alliance by both countries, Seoul has had the bitter experience of being largely ignored as Washington dealt with important issues affecting Korean national interests. Bush's "axis of evil" statement is only the most recent example; the Clinton administration's treatment of the North Korean nuclear issue in the mid-1990s is another. Seoul was largely left out of the decisionmaking process as Washington was pursuing bilateral negotiations with Pyongyang to prevent it from developing nuclear weapons. This omission insulted many in the South and angered a great number of otherwise pro-American conservatives.

U.S. disloyalty

Moreover, scarring episodes of U.S. disloyalty reach even further back than the last decade. In 1905, through a secret agreement between U.S. secretary of war William H. Taft and imperial Japan's Prime Minister Count Katsura Taro, Koreans believe that the United States sold out Korea to Japan by approving Japan's domination over Korea in return for Japanese approval of U.S. domination in the Philippines. The United States blatantly disregarded the 1882 bilateral U.S.-Korean treaty, in which the United States promised to provide "good offices" in the event of an external threat.

> *Younger Koreans increasingly want to see a significant reduction of U.S. forces in South Korea or even a complete withdrawal.*

Many Korean intellectuals also believe that the United States holds responsibility both for the outbreak of the Korean War (1950–1953) and the division of Korea. In their view, Korea's division was driven by U.S. suppression of popular and leftist movements during the military occupation of 1945–1948. Then, the withdrawal of U.S. troops from South Korea in 1949, followed by then–Secretary of State Dean Acheson's announcement in January 1950 that South Korea would be outside the

U.S. defense perimeter in the Asia-Pacific region, openly invited Communist aggression from the North in June 1950. Yet, at the same time, they appreciate and recognize the United States as a liberator after World War II and as their savior during the Korean War. Today, however, Koreans are skeptical and believe that, if necessary, the United States may abandon South Korea again in favor of U.S. global strategic interests.

> *Korean attitudes toward the United States in turn reverberate back through U.S. attitudes toward South Korea.*

A rise in anti-Americanism might be a component in the natural path of South Korea's graduation from a client state to a dynamic and vibrant member of the international community. Korean self-confidence and national pride have grown commensurately with increasing sophistication, economic success, and international prestige exemplified by its membership in the Organization of Economic Cooperation and Development, its growth into the twelfth-largest economy in the world, its hosting the 1988 Summer Olympics, and its cohosting the 2002 World Cup with Japan. These developments have led Koreans to question some of the country's past practices, values, and relationships; to seek greater political and security independence from the United States; and to demand a more equal partnership and mutual respect in the bilateral relationship.

To be fair, however, anti-Americanism is probably rising because nationalism is increasing both in South Korea and the United States. U.S. nationalism is influenced by the country's status as the sole global superpower, while Korean nationalism grows as the country becomes more industrialized. Koreans are satisfied with an alliance with the United States as well as with U.S. leadership in the international community, but they increasingly emphasize the value of national pride, equality in the relationship, and greater independence from the United States.

How low can we go?

Looking ahead, anti-Americanism in South Korea is unlikely to disappear. It has been accumulating over the protracted period of the bilateral relationship, and its causes are too complex to be resolved overnight. The level of anti-American sentiment is expected to fluctuate with events over time. Current trends suggest the great possibility that South Korea's resentment toward the United States will become more aggravated in coming years. Despite the long history of the alliance, the discrepancy between both countries' national strengths and goals could lead to a serious conflict of interests at the same time that cultural and conceptual differences continue to cause emotional resentment. . . .

Korean attitudes toward the United States in turn reverberate back through U.S. attitudes toward South Korea. The rise of anti-American sentiment in South Korea only means that U.S. resentment toward South Korea will likely grow in response to negative Korean attitudes and policies. This dynamic has the potential to become a dangerous, downward spiral of increasing tensions between populations and even governments. An escalating clash between anti-Americanism in South Korea and anti-Koreanism in the United States could undermine the U.S.-Korean alliance—exactly what the North Korean leadership would like to see.

> **// *The United States and South Korea share responsibility for the rise of anti-Americanism. //***

Some U.S. citizens feel that the Korean public has unfairly blamed the United States for no apparent reason, as was the case in the gold medal controversy in Utah. In recent years, benign U.S. policies seem to have gone unappreciated in South Korea. The United States has served as a shield to protect South Korea over the past five decades in accordance with the 1954 Mutual Defense Treaty. Yet, when terrorists threatened U.S. security, South Korea's political leadership and the Korean people provided lukewarm support in response to the U.S. request for help.

The future of the U.S.-Korean alliance is too important for Washington and Seoul to overlook this current trend of rising anti-Americanism and the potential rise of anti-Koreanism, as they directly threaten the special U.S.-ROK symbiotic relationship. The alliance with the United States is critical for South Korea to preserve stability on the peninsula and in the region.

In addition, Korean instability that could arise in the absence of a U.S. security commitment would complicate Korean efforts to sustain current and expected levels of foreign investments throughout the country, thus threatening continued economic progress. Regional stability is also critical for South Korea because it conducts more than two-thirds of its trade in the Asia-Pacific region, with the volume of current South Korean trade through Asian naval transport routes exceeding 40 percent of its total trade. Even after unification, South Korea's alliance with the United States will continue to be important to protect the peninsula from once again becoming the political, if not the military, battleground where the major Asian powers have historically sought regional hegemony.

> *The bottom line still remains that the well-being of the U.S.-Korean alliance is crucial for both countries.*

The alliance with South Korea is also critical for the United States to maintain its leadership position in the Asia-Pacific region. The partnership helps prevent the eruption of hostilities on the Korean peninsula, which could otherwise draw China into a reenactment of the Korean War. It helps preserve a stable balance of power in the region by hedging against the rise of an aggressive regional power and regional rivalries, and it helps protect U.S. economic interests. More than one-third of total U.S. trade is conducted with the Asia-Pacific region, and millions of U.S. jobs would be at stake if continued regional growth and development were jeopardized.

Stemming the tide of discontent

The United States and South Korea share responsibility for the rise of anti-Americanism. As long as the U.S.-ROK alliance proves to be critical to both sides, however, orchestrated efforts by the two countries are both possible and essential to counter this trend. A perfect cure might not exist, as some of the problems—manifested in things such as the Winter Olympics and late-night TV banter—are beyond the control of either side. Nevertheless, measures can be taken to halt and abate the current trend of anti-American sentiments. . . .

To alleviate, or at least abate, the policy-driven and emotional causes of anti-Americanism, Washington must take the aspirations of the Korean people into account in the bilateral relationship. In dealing with South Korea, the United States should reflect on the following points:

- The Korean people cherish and place a high value on respect; therefore, actions that demonstrate U.S. respect for Koreans, whether genuine or not, may be the secret to improving the U.S. image in South Korea substantially. . . .
- The United States must give Koreans reason to believe that, as a committed ally and friend, it will not sacrifice South Korea under any possible circumstances in favor of U.S. interests. To counter lingering negative feelings from past incidents . . . Washington should maintain close consultation and cooperation with Seoul on any matters or issues regarding U.S.-Korean relations.
- A clearer understanding of how Koreans think and what Koreans need is critical for the United States. This knowledge will help prevent cultural and conceptual differences and misunderstandings from leading Koreans to blame the United States for problems that arise, even with no reason to do so. Koreans are emotional, and their attitudes are strongly influenced by the concept of *ki-bun*—a combination of mood, feelings, and emotions. The concept of *che-myon*—a combination of dignity, pride, and honor—is another important factor. The traditional Korean culture places an enormous value on these two ideas. No matter how generous and cautious the United States is toward Korea, the relationship may eventually become disastrous if U.S. policy and actions hurt Koreans' *ki-bun* and *che-myon*. Korean attitudes toward the United States are likely to improve dramatically if Americans are able to understand and be aware of these factors behind Korean sentiment.

Improving the U.S. image

Overall, a public outreach campaign conducted by both the U.S. government and the private sector may be instrumental to improving the image of the United States and deterring anti-American sentiments from rising based on emotional sources. Public outreach efforts should have two primary targets: (1) the Korean broadcasting networks, newspapers, and opinion makers at large; and (2) the younger generations, particularly those between their twenties and forties. U.S. efforts to explain the concerns and intentions underlying U.S. government policies and actions to the Korean public will go a long way toward deterring further misunderstandings and bringing about a more positive perception of the United States.

Korean newspapers and broadcast networks are key vehicles for shaping public opinion; they thereby have a responsibility to be fair, objective, and unbiased. Instead of getting caught up in an emotional rage, the Korean media should keep in mind the importance of not only the symbiotic relationship between the United States and South Korea but also of Korean national interests. Most crucially, the media must make every effort to present both sides of the story and help create a more favorable environment to improve U.S.-Korean relations and a more positive image of the United States in South Korea.

Along with U.S. efforts to present a more positive image, the Korean government should take the lead in improving the image of the United States by providing accurate information and advice to the media as well as the public. A key message— and one that should be highlighted—is the importance of national interests and the strategic and economic implications of growing anti-Americanism in South Korea. . . .

The bottom line still remains that the well-being of the U.S.-Korean alliance is crucial for both countries. Both governments are responsible for understanding this importance, educating the public, and taking courses of action to maintain and improve the bilateral relationship. Although Koreans emotionally feel bitter toward the United States, an underlying respect for Americans and their culture still exists, evident in the Korean saying, "Yankee go home, but take me with you." This respect must be tapped so that all can benefit.

7

Anti-Americanism Is a Minority View

Economist

The Economist *is a weekly newspaper that provides analysis of world business and current affairs.*

While anti-Americanism around the world has risen slightly, it is still a minority point of view. Surveys show that the majority of countries hold favorable opinions of the United States and share with America common values and goals. However, America must not take this support for granted; if it fails to nurture its international friendships, it could see increasing dislike from other countries. Since the United States will have difficulty achieving its future goals without international cooperation, it is important that it work to maintain the current goodwill it has from other countries.

Criticism of America is inevitable and even healthy—but don't let it get out of hand.

Dealing with North Korea and Iraq, along with assorted other problems of international affairs, will be hard enough. Dealing with the apparent tide of anti-American feeling around the globe promises to be an even harder task during 2003. Even in South Korea, protected as it has been from a hostile North by American forces and friendship for half a century, the news that its brutal, dictatorial neighbour was playing nuclear games was taken as a cue for street protests against the United States for having supposedly provoked the North by its tough line against it. Meanwhile, in Europe and in parts of the Arab world, it was being criticised for taking a softer line on

North Korea than on Iraq. No radio phone-in on world affairs is complete, even in friendly Britain, without callers accusing America of being reckless, bullying, unprincipled, ideologically-driven (ie, too principled), greedy for oil, Zionist, led by a moron, led by a Machiavellian election-stealing dictator . . . and countless other accusations.

Wide but not deep

Anti-Americanism is real and has been growing ever since the September 11th (2001) attacks, not because of those attacks but because America has, since then, been using or talking about using military force. It is harder, though, to gauge the trend's significance. In part, it is just the unhappy lot of the happy leader. "Envy is a worm that does not rest, it is the cause of the resentment and hatred shown to us by Turks, Arabs, Jews, French, Italians, Germans, Czechs, English and Scots." Thus a Spanish soldier writing in the 1580s, when his country was the world's hyperpower; but it could just as easily have been a Briton in the 19th century or a Roman in the second. Now it is America's turn, as in truth it has been ever since the Aldermaston anti-nuke march,[1] Vietnam and the cruise-missile controversy during the cold war. And America gives as good as it gets, especially since the shock of the Twin Towers. Europeans, it is often said, are on another planet; they have no moral compass; they are appeasers and freeloaders; and, because they so often criticise Israel too, they are anti-Semitic.

> ❝ *The values of America and most of its allies are not, in truth, that different and the dislikes not deep.* ❞

Moreover, although the trend may be unfavourable, its scale does not yet look daunting. The values of America and most of its allies are not, in truth, that different and the dislikes not deep. Recent opinion surveys do show that anti-Americanism has risen. But it is still a minority point of view. In one recent audit of people in 42 countries by the Pew Research Centre,

1. the 1959 march from London to Aldermaston to protest nuclear weapons

America was looked on favourably by most people in 35 of them (a superpower batting average that would have been beyond Spain in the 16th century). Most people among America's allies support the war on terror; most admire its culture; and nearly all of them would feel less safe if there were another superpower to challenge it.

This admiration has practical consequences. Despite the protests in the streets, leaders in most countries have gone along with America's policies since September 11th. When [U.S president George W. Bush] took the issue of Iraq to the UN [United Nations] Security Council, he received (eventually) unanimous support. When he "arogantly" revoked the Anti-Ballistic Missile Treaty, Russia and China gave their consent. America has 17 fully-fledged military bases beyond its borders, thanks to many countries being happy to play host to them. When push comes to shove, America has generally got what it wanted from its allies, not just because it is so much stronger militarily, but because, as Mr Bush has put it, there are "common values of freedom, human rights and democracy". In the end—or even in the beginning—other countries tend to want what America wants, and to trust it, more or less, to do the right thing.

Friendships still need nurturing

The question, though, is whether this can be taken for granted or whether a time might soon come when the alignment of wants, or the trust, might collapse. It is an odd question to have to pose, right now, in 2003. During the cold war, America was quite often brusque and unprincipled in pursuit of its basic goal—the defeat, or holding at bay, of communism. It continues to be criticised for things it did and dictators it supported 20, 30 or even 40 years ago, as if nothing had changed in the meantime. But it has: since the end of the cold war democracy has spread widely and American policy has become more plainly directed at human rights and democracy than ever before. Mr Bush's speeches, indeed, have echoed the idealistic, human rights-oriented words of [former U.S. president] Woodrow Wilson more than have those of most other recent presidents. At the level of values there seems now to be less of a divide, not more.

Two aspects of the United States make that judgment inadequate, however: one cultural, the other political. The opinion surveys analysed in our special report show that although

America, Europe and other allies do share common values, America is an outlier among the rich countries in terms of its religiosity, patriotism and traditionalism. Most European countries, and Japan too, have become more secular in recent years. America has become more traditional. Far from uniting the old allies, in other words, Mr Bush's Wilsonianism may help to divide them; although Europeans agree with his ends, many feel uncomfortable with the fervour and moral idealism that—they fear—determine the means.

> **America needs its leaders to bend over backwards to nurture its friendships and to show that other people's views matter.**

The political aspect is more secular: America's constitutional system of divided government, combined with its belief in pluralism and free speech. These mean that not only is political debate in America more often about values and morals than it is in Europe but also that all political debate is noisier and more confusing. Washington is full of voices saying all sorts of different things, many within the same party, some even within the same administration. Critics, or just the plain scared, among its allies can always find somebody who has just said something that they find objectionable.

This, combined with the revived use by America of military power since September 11th, may explain why anti-American sentiment has grown. The main solution to it will lie in successful actions that prove—or reconfirm—that American ends are good and its methods sound. But it is not enough to shrug and wait for that joyous feeling of vindication. For anti-American sentiment matters because America cannot achieve its ends on its own. The danger is that more allied leaders will follow [German chancellor] Gerhard Schroeder's example in [2002's] German election and decide that anti-American opinion among swing voters can be exploited politically—which, in turn, could help thwart the very actions, in Iraq, the Middle East, Central Asia, Korea and elsewhere, that America needs to pull off if it is to convince its critics.

The implication may be galling for some in Washington, but it is clear. Even when it feels it is plainly in the right, the superpower needs to make a greater effort to consult its allies and persuade them to support it. And it must do so publicly, in full view of public opinion, rather than merely through private phone calls between the world's capitals or by granting audiences in Washington. It is a new form of the old principle of noblesse oblige: in its own interests, America needs its leaders to bend over backwards to nurture its friendships and to show that other people's views matter. As long as their help matters, there is no real alternative.

8

America's War on Terrorism Has Provoked International Resentment

Lutz Kleveman

Lutz Kleveman is the author of The New Great Game: Blood and Oil in Central Asia.

America's war on terrorism has provoked international hatred for the United States. U.S. mistreatment of Iraqis during the 2003 Iraq war has provoked the populace there to show increasing support for anti-American terrorists. Indeed, America's policies, which many people believe are hypocritical, have provoked hatred for the United States in many parts of the world. By alienating other nations and leaving those it has invaded in economic ruin, the United States is creating fertile ground for terrorists to operate.

The day after US army soldiers in Iraq shot Yaass Abbass dead [during the 2003 war to depose Saddam Hussein] I realised why America was losing the war on terror. The 28-year-old truck driver from Fallujah, a centre of Iraqi guerrilla resistance west of Baghdad, had been innocent, but that was not the point. Nor was the sobbing of his five orphaned sons during the family's mourning ceremony in a hastily set-up tent. Nor even the out-

Lutz Kleveman, "How America Makes Terrorists of Its Allies: Kudair Abbass Was Happy to See the U.S. Army Keeping Peace in Iraq—Until Troops Killed His Brother for Violating the Curfew. Now, Like So Many in the Region, He Wants Revenge," *New Statesman*, vol. 132, October 13, 2003. Copyright © 2003 by New Statesman, Ltd. Reproduced by permission.

rage of the tribal representatives who arrived to offer condolences, shrouded in white dishdasha robes and turbans. What struck me was the US air force Apache combat helicopter, which kept hovering above the tent, the engines' roaring noise drowning out the men's recital of verses from the Koran.

"The Americans treat us like animals," said Kudair Abbass, one of Yaass's brothers. When asked if he wanted revenge, he kept silent but his eyes, filled with tears and hate, gave a clear answer. And it had nothing to do with any loyalty to Saddam Hussein.

Growing support for terrorists

Where do local people stand in the war on terror? This is what I tried to find out on numerous journeys through the Middle East, the Caucasus and central Asia [between 2001 and 2003]. Certainly, the anti-terrorism struggle has had successes. Since [the terrorist attacks of] 11 September 2001, no major terrorist attack has occurred on American or European soil. But [terrorist] Osama Bin Laden takes afternoon strolls in the Afghan-Pakistani borderlands; in southern Afghanistan, the Taliban [which aided al-Qaeda terrorists] are on the rebound; and "liberated" Iraq sinks further into violence and lawlessness each day. There have been tactical mistakes, such as letting Bin Laden slip away from Tora Bora [Afghanistan] two years ago; but equally to blame are strategic failures, such as neglecting the Israeli-Palestinian conflict and making terrorist sponsoring Saudi Arabia and Pakistan "allies" in a struggle against evil that they themselves support. Worse, in stubbornly going it alone against Iraq, the US has lost many allies in a war that cannot be won unilaterally.

The growing popular support some terrorists enjoy is too often ignored. Bin Laden and the Iraqi bombers can cause harm only so long as people give them shelter. And many Muslims do, because they see America's war on terror as a crusade against Islam.

What makes a man a terrorist? On my travels, I met countless angry (mostly young) men who, with nothing to lose but their seemingly valueless lives, were prepared to fight for whatever their leaders told them was worth the fight. Among them were Kudair from Iraq, Ahmad from Uzbekistan and Kamal By from Afghanistan. Each demonstrates in his own different way why the Bush administration's anti-terror strategy is going awry.

"Yaass just wanted to get some gasoline in town," his brother Kudair said. "The curfew was near but he did not care." Then his old Volkswagen broke down and Yaass had to repair it in the dark. Around midnight, a US army Humvee patrol came driving towards him. The soldiers of an elite squad of the 3rd Infantry Division were in Fallujah following a series of guerrilla attacks. They were originally trained not as policemen, but to kill people. They were tired and aggressive. "They just shot my brother dead, for no reason," Kudair exclaimed. As several witnesses attested, Yaass had been unarmed. "He was not a resistance fighter but a simple civilian who worked hard to feed his family." Had the Americans offered any explanation for the killing? "Of course not. We don't even exist for them. They have not liberated us, not us." There seemed little point in asking Kudair what he would do if any guerrilla groups asked him to join their struggle.

> *In stubbornly going it alone against Iraq, the US has lost many allies in a war that cannot be won unilaterally.*

Fallujah was only one destination on a four-week journey through post-Saddam Iraq that took me from Baghdad to the Kurdish areas in the north, the Shia cities in the south, and the Sunni triangle in the west. While the Kurds were unreservedly happy about having been liberated from the tyrant, any gratitude felt by Shias or Sunnis has long since been replaced by resentment that the heavy handed military occupiers seem incapable (and unwilling) to embark on the necessary reconstruction effort. In Baghdad, there is still no regular supply of electricity and water, and crime is on the rise, an environment perfect for terrorists. The irony is that, by invading Iraq without clear ideas of what to do after a ceasefire, the Bush administration has created what it set out to destroy: a terrorist haven.

Anti-terrorist policies cause hatred

Iraq is not the only country where US anti-terrorist policies have backfired. In the ex-Soviet republic of Uzbekistan, in central Asia, the brutal dictator Islam Karimov has become an ally of Washington's in the war on terror, allowing American troops to set up a large and permanent US base on Uzbek soil during the Afghan campaign [to oust the Taliban in 2001]. In the capital, Tashkent, I met 20-year-old Ahmad. Over a cup of tea, the young man told me he had just been released from prison; he served three years for allegedly belonging to an Islamic terrorist organization. "The guards beat me every day," Ahmad said, "but I never stopped praying to Allah."

The group he belonged to was a Sufi religious order which, he insisted, had nothing to do with terrorists such as the Islamic Movement of Uzbekistan, blamed for several deadly attacks in the late 1990s. "But maybe in the future my brothers and I will have to defend ourselves and fight," he said. I asked Ahmad how he felt about the arrival of American anti-terror troops in Uzbekistan. "They only make things worse. They don't help us, the people, but only the government. I hate America."

Ahmad's angry words reflect many central Asians' deep suspicion of US motives in their region. The Caspian Basin harbours the greatest untapped oil reserves in the world, which could help industrialised countries decrease their dependence on oil from the volatile Middle East. In this new great game that pits the US against Russia, China and Iran, the Bush administration has used the war on terror to expand its military presence and political influence in central Asia.

Criticisms of American foreign policy

Cynicism over America's energy imperialism could ultimately deride the outcome of the war on terror. The impoverished people of the region, disgusted with the US alliances with their corrupt and despotic rulers, increasingly embrace militant Islam and virulent anti-Americanism. At the end of the cold war in 1989, America was admired and loved by the Soviet-oppressed peoples of eastern Europe not only as the leader of "the west" but as the champion of democracy, civil liberties and cultural progress. Young Czechs, Poles and Hungarians, even if they had never heard of the Bill of Rights, craved American rock music and blue jeans. Since the current Bush administration turned the 11 September terror attacks into an excuse to pursue policies seen by many as arrogant, aggressive and imperialist, the change in perception could not be more drastic. The US has lost most of its cultural attractiveness in the ex-Soviet countries of central Asia and their neighbours, and is widely hated for its politics.

Many have come to realise that the democratic and liberal values Americans enjoy at home are often missing from US foreign policy. They resent the immoral opportunism with which Washington courts the region's dictators, such as Karimov, Azerbaijan's Heydar Aliyev, Kazakhstan's Nursultan Nazarbayev and Pakistan's Pervez Musharraf. Such alliances serve short-term interests but in the long run are likely to exacerbate the problem.

> *Many have come to realise that the democratic and liberal values Americans enjoy at home are often missing from US foreign policy.*

In Afghanistan, too, the Bush administration has made Faustian pacts. [In 2003,] two years after Operation Enduring Freedom, most of the country has sunk back into chaos and anarchy, ruled by warlords who defy Hamid Karzai's weak central government. The Taliban and the mujahedin of the radical Islamist Gulbuddin Hekmatyar are staging a violent comeback, drawing US and allied troops deeper into counter-insurgency warfare. The only flourishing business is the export of opium and heroin which, according to UN statistics, has increased twentyfold since the fall of the Taliban [in 2001].

Kamal By, a poppy farmer whom I met in the lawless northeast province of Badakhshan, reached under his shalwar kameez, pulled out a sticky lump of recently harvested opium and whispered: "This stuff is good—the dealers on the bazaar are wild about it. They give me $350 per kilo." Farmers in his village have little choice but to grow poppy. Other crops yield a fraction of the profits and, said Kamal By: "The warlords force us to grow poppy. We have to pay them the ushr, one-tenth of our profits. In the west, you are upset about the opium we produce. But where do the weapons come from with which the warlords suppress us here?"

In search of temporary allies against the Taliban and al-Qaeda, the CIA [Central Intelligence Agency] still bankrolls Afghan warlords, including some notorious heroin dealers. Compounded by Washington's failure at postwar nation-building, this exacerbates chaos and civil strife, once again creating a breeding ground for terrorism instead of obliterating it. The US is repeating mistakes of the 1980s, when the CIA supported Islamic radicals such as Hekmatyar and a certain Osama Bin Laden in the anti-Soviet jihad.

The need to win hearts and minds

The stories of Kudair, Ahmad and Kamal By reveal the myopia of US tactics. Final victory in the war on terror cannot be achieved by military means alone; it also demands political and economic measures that target the social roots of terrorism. B-52s [bombers] and cruise missiles inspire fear and hatred, but building more roads, schools and hospitals would win hearts and minds.

Why do so many people hate America? "They hate our freedom and democracy," said President [George W.] Bush. That may be true of a few, but most America-haters have better reasons.

In late March [2003] right after the invasion of Iraq, I asked Richard Perle, a leading pro-war voice in Washington, if the rise of anti-Americanism, particularly in Afghanistan and Pakistan, threatened the war on terror. "I don't see why bringing freedom to the Iraqi people would inspire people to take up arms against the United States," Perle replied. "Frankly, I don't see why our success in the war on terror is dependent on the goodwill of the Afghan or the Pakistani population. I think there will be a sharply reduced danger of terrorism after this war."

Sadly, wishful thinking alone rarely guarantees success.

9

There Is No Evidence That America's Response to Terrorism Has Provoked International Resentment

Gerard Alexander

Gerard Alexander is an associate professor of politics at the University of Virginia and author of The Sources of Democratic Consolidation.

Many critics charge that America's shift to a more aggressive foreign policy after the September 11, 2001, terrorist attacks has caused international fear and resentment, and is endangering American interests. If this was true, there should be evidence of balancing—when countries expand their militaries and seek allies in response to a perceived threat. However, there is no evidence of this balancing behavior against America. Recent international conflicts are simply the result of routine diplomatic friction. Due to this lack of evidence that U.S. foreign policy has bred global resentment, America should continue with its war on terrorism in order to effectively protect itself.

The Bush administration's foreign policy has come under withering attack in [late 2003]. Critics accuse the administration of crossing the line that separates a foreign policy strong enough to secure U.S. interests from one so muscular that it pro-

Gerard Alexander, "An Unbalanced Critique of Bush: What the International Relations Experts Get Wrong," *Weekly Standard*, November 3, 2003, pp. 25–29.

vokes other countries to block us instead. The charge boils down to this: Bush is creating new enemies faster than he is deterring old ones.

If this line of criticism is correct, then many conservative assumptions about foreign policy may be dangerously flawed. Conservative hawks want to vigorously pursue U.S. security in a world of new and uncertain dangers. But they have no desire to do it so zealously that they cause a self-defeating backlash. In this, they have no better authority than George W. Bush, who said in 2000 that if "we're an arrogant nation, they'll resent us."

> *American forces have been committed to Europe or Asia only when an aggressor threatened to dominate those regions, and only in cooperation with local allies.*

The problem is that it's unclear where the line is drawn. A vocal minority claims that U.S. "aggression" has provoked worldwide resentment and "blowback," including [the September 11, 2001, terrorist attack] itself. But most American observers would disagree, insisting that this country is unthreatening when compared to almost all other great powers of history, which is why the United States has provoked so little animosity. Theorists of the "realist" school of international relations explain this by describing the United States as an "offshore balancer." In this view, American forces have been committed to Europe or Asia only when an aggressor threatened to dominate those regions, and only in cooperation with local allies. Because U.S. forces were clearly there not by choice and not to stay, American intervention was generally welcomed. Whatever the reasons for its restraint, America's behavior was unlike that of normal great powers. Others detected that difference, and responded accordingly: Whereas they "balanced" against other great powers by expanding their militaries and seeking allies, America provoked very little balancing.

Balancing against the United States

This view survived well after America emerged as the sole superpower. As recently as May 2000, prominent international relations scholars met to try to explain why countries were still not balancing against the United States. Stephen Walt, a prominent realist and a dean of Harvard's Kennedy School, described this absence in a chapter of the book *America Unrivaled:*

> Disagreements and policy disputes are hardly a new development in U.S. relations with its principal allies, yet there have been no significant defections [from U.S. alliances] in the ten years since the Soviet Union imploded. Russia, China, North Korea, and a few others have occasionally collaborated . . . but their efforts fall well short of formal defense arrangements. . . . [U.S.] allies may resent their dependence on the United States and complain about erratic U.S. leadership, but the old cry of "Yankee, Go Home" is strikingly absent in Europe and Asia. . . . No one is making a serious effort to forge a meaningful anti-American alliance.

Walt concluded that "balancing tendencies—while they do exist—are remarkably mild. It is possible to find them, but one has to squint pretty hard."

In the past 18 months, hawks have been bombarded with warnings that squinting is no longer needed. They are being warned that the Bush administration's policies are likely to provoke other countries to frustrate our goals rather than help us achieve them. The result would be diminished rather than enhanced U.S. security. The *New York Times* has editorialized that Bush's "lone-wolf record" and "overly aggressive stance" risk "undermining the very interests that Mr. Bush seeks to protect" by inspiring "the enmity rather than the envy of the world." This has become practically the official foreign policy stance of numerous intellectuals and commentators, the AFL-CIO, and the entire Democratic presidential pack.

It is also echoed by usually sober international relations scholars. The University of Chicago's Robert Pape argues that the administration's "threat to wage unilateral preventive war" crucially "changed America's long-enjoyed reputation for benign intent" and is inspiring others to balance against the United States. Stephen Walt says that Washington today [in 2003] is in the position of imperial Germany in the two-decade lead-up to 1914, when that country's expansionism caused "its own encirclement." Chicago's John Mearsheimer joined Walt this past winter [2002] to argue that the proposed Iraq operation was likely to "reinforce the growing perception that the United States is a bully." Each was among the nearly three dozen international relations scholars who warned in an open letter in the *New York Times* that the Iraq war would provoke "increasing anti-Americanism" worldwide.

Change in U.S. policy

These critics link three basic claims. The United States traditionally gained cooperation by being unthreatening. The Bush administration is departing sharply from that tradition. And this convergence with the behavior of normal great powers is causing other countries to begin balancing against us. In yet another way, history is back, except this time we are inflicting it on ourselves.

What do these critics believe is causing this seismic shift? Even before September 11, 2001, the Bush administration "unilaterally" rejected four treaties or near-agreements. It withdrew from the ABM [Anti-Ballistic Missile Treaty] treaty and began deploying a provocative missile defense. It expanded NATO [North Atlantic Treaty Organization] up to Russia's borders. After September 11, it invested heavily in power-projection capabilities. Bush's 2002 *National Security Strategy* called for the United States to make "preventive" war and declared it a primary U.S. goal to prevent any other country from developing the military resources to rival us. Consistent with that doctrine, the United States invaded Iraq [in 2003] over the stated opposition of most governments.

> *Critics say . . . fears of America are already being translated into balancing actions against the United States.*

Hawkish conservatives believe these policies represent no more than a robust protection of national security in the face of new threats. But that would be of small comfort if others perceive them as threatening and balance against us as a result. How do we decide who is right? The critics claim the verdict is already in, and that it favors them.

Their evidence comes in two forms. First, the showcase rising criticism of the United States as revealed in public opinion surveys, especially the ubiquitous Pew Research Center's 2002 polls conducted in 44 countries. These surveys show that high and rising percentages of people in many countries have "unfavorable" views of America, believe the United States is unilateralist, and are increasingly prone to fearing the U.S. could threaten their country. . . .

Second, critics say these fears of America are already being translated into balancing actions against the United States. Most concretely, many countries refused either to endorse the invasion of Iraq, vote with the United States in the U.N. [United Nations] Security Council, or offer military bases. France, Germany, Russia, and China cooperated in resisting Washington's designs. . . .

Routine diplomatic friction

If this is true, hawks should be worried that overreaching is endangering American interests. But how persuasive is this evidence? It certainly doesn't meet the standards set by international relations theorists in the past. In their own major research, for example, Walt and Mearsheimer judge that balancing behavior has occurred when countries (in Mearsheimer's words) "invest heavily in defense," transforming latent power into military capabilities; or seek explicit military alliances; or "send clear signals to the aggressor" that they are willing to take costly actions to maintain the existing balance of power. These are commonly accepted standards for measuring balancing behavior in the study of international relations. And for good reason: These muscular actions can easily be distinguished from the diplomatic friction that routinely occurs between almost all countries, even allies.

The problem with the recent criticisms is that the combination of unfavorable polls and diplomatic maneuvering falls well short of these standards. A number of critics appear to recognize this, since they describe what they now see as "soft" balancing, or "surreptitious" balancing, or "neo-" or "proto-" or "pre-" balancing behavior, instead of balancing plain and simple, or what you might call balancing without adjectives. But it is not clear that "soft balancing" is distinguishable from garden variety diplomatic friction.

We can easily look back at periods in which everyone agrees the United States was *not* being balanced against, and find events that were every bit as serious as those of the past 18 months. . . .

Few analysts conclude that these earlier events represented balancing against the United States. Yet they either parallel or exceed in seriousness the events that critics (sometimes the same analysts) now identify as balancing behavior. In many cases the events cited to criticize the Bush administration are simply extrapolations of earlier trends. These include:

- the formation of the European Union (initially launched in 1952), and Europe's common currency (agreed to in 1993)
- waves of extensive anti-Americanism (pervasive in Latin America in the 1950s and '60s, and Europe and elsewhere in the late 1960s and early '70s)
- China's rapid military buildup (begun at least in the early 1990s)
- Russia, France, and China's policy of blocking serious U.N.-sanctioned use of force against Saddam (demonstrable since the mid-1990s)
- the Russia-China "strategic partnership" (declared in 1996)
- the "European troika" meetings and agreements between Germany, France, and Russia (begun in 1998)
- creation of an independent, unified European military force (first negotiated in 1952 and agreed to in 1998).

Obviously the same events can mean different things in different contexts. But unless it is made clear why these events did not constitute balancing before but do now, they are simply not persuasive evidence of American overreach.

> *In many cases the events cited to criticize the Bush administration are simply extrapolations of earlier trends.*

If we really want to test whether America's post-9/11 foreign policy is provoking even incipient balancing behavior, we have to look for events that *can* be clearly distinguished from routine diplomatic friction. What does balancing plain and simple look like? International relations theorists generally have relied on two main types of evidence: "internal balancing"—higher defense budgets, troop call-ups—and "external balancing," or alliance building.

Types of balancing

Internal balancing against a country as powerful as the United States wouldn't come cheap or easy. Trends in military spending—steeper and more durable drops in Europe and Russia since the end of the Cold War than in the United States—have resulted in a widening American lead in military technology and power projection capabilities. Even Europe's sophisticated militaries lack independent command, intelligence, surveillance, and logistical capabilities. Russia, China, and others are even less able to match the United States militarily. But in the aggregate, these disparities are the result of budgetary choices, not rigid constraints. [Historian] Samuel Huntington calls the current world system "a uni-multipolar system with one superpower and several major powers." Those several major powers have latent capabilities that could be mobilized and aggregated to check the United States.

Consider the latent potential of Western Europe alone. The E.U. members jointly have more troops under arms than the United States (about 1.8 to 1.4 million). They have the organizational and technical skills to excel at command, control, and surveillance. They have the know-how to develop a wide range of high-tech weapons. And they have the money to pay for them, with a total GDP of almost $8 trillion to the U.S.'s $10 trillion. This is before we consider Japan's wealth and technology, China's manpower, and Russia's extensive arms production capacities.

These potentialities could also be exploited through alliances—external balancing. Forming alliances imposes costs; the more partners needed, the higher those costs can be, and some countries prefer to free ride. But here, too, the costs are by no means unprecedented. The tightly interwoven E.U. members can coordinate at lower cost than almost any alliance in history. The addition to them of Russia and China would create an alliance with huge capabilities and global presence.

No evidence of balancing

The question is whether we can see evidence of such internal and external balancing. The answer is no.

There is a long history of countries making dogged attempts to catch up, sometimes at great cost, when they feel threatened by more advanced rivals. Such build-ups can be slow to start and gather momentum. But it is when they are underway that we know internal balancing is occurring. This contrasts starkly with today's record of mobilization. China and many countries in the Middle East and sub-Saharan Africa are increasing military spending. But for the most part, they have been doing so for years or decades. Most other countries are also maintaining their pre-Bush trajectories in military spending, and those trajectories are flat.

This is especially visible in Europe. If diplomatic opposition over [the 2003 war in] Iraq and rising suspicion and unfavorable images of the United States are valid indicators of incipient balancing behavior, then Europe is a prime place to look for follow-through. After all, Germany and France were among the most prominent opponents of the war, with France serving as the most active balancing "entrepreneur," lobbying other countries to deny Washington their cooperation. Yet there is little evidence that a build-up, as a hedge against future American actions, is even in its earliest stages. . . .

Only France meets the dual criteria of a would-be balancer that has moved to beef up its defense spending since the lead-up to the Iraq war—from a low of 1.9 percent of GDP in 2001–2 to a projected 2.5 percent. But without matching performance by Germany and others, France's effort is isolated. And if French assertiveness alone were used as evidence of American overreach, then every U.S. administration since 1945 would have to be judged guilty.

> // *There is little evidence that a build-up, as a hedge against future American actions, is even in its earliest stages.* //

The recent [2000] launch of a unified E.U. military force only reinforces the impression of a broad European non-response to the Bush strategy. This force of 60,000 is designed for light, rapid deployment to zones like the Balkans and is totally unsuited to continental defense. It is designed to balance against the [European dictators] of this world, not the Americans.

Maybe Europeans can't spend more on their militaries, however much they might want to, because their welfare states are expensive and they agreed to strict budget deficit limits for the euro. If that's the case, they must believe that maintaining generous entitlements and adhering to technical aspects of their common currency are higher priorities than generating defenses against a potential U.S. threat. At worst, Europeans could upgrade by simply reallocating spending away from foreign aid. They aren't doing that either. It is as if, despite the rhetoric, they don't actually believe the United States might threaten them.

This disparity between rhetoric and follow-through is brought into high relief when Europe is compared with America, which *has* genuinely felt threatened since September 11, 2001. The United States has begun a formidable military build-up. This (among other things) has contributed to a deterioration from budget surpluses to deficits. But most Americans appear to accept this as a price worth paying. So far, Europeans show little comparable interest in reshuffling priorities.

> *Unfavorable surveys and diplomatic friction there may be, but they are not being followed up with actual balancing behavior.*

A similar pattern can be seen in alliance-building: Unfavorable surveys and diplomatic friction there may be, but they are not being followed up with actual balancing behavior. In the past, threats have commonly led to substantive alliances of coordination and mutual defense. At times, this required countries to set aside old animosities, as [former U.S. president] Richard Nixon and [former Chinese leader] Mao Zedong could attest. But today [2003], even with an alliance facilitator available—[French president] Jacques Chirac's France—there is little visible change in the alliance patterns of the late 1990s. Russia-China relations still "fall well short of formal defense arrangements" (to cite Stephen Walt). The E.U. has barely more of a common defense policy than before. As international relations theorist Robert Lieber notes, NATO is expanding and thriving instead of withering. There is no evidence that cooperation between major E.U. members and Russia (or China) extends to anything beyond opposition to an invasion already over. In the Muslim world, several states prominently cooperated with that invasion. At least for now, diplomacy is strictly at the level of maneuvering and talk, indistinguishable from the friction common to virtually all periods and countries, even allies.

Erring on the side of caution

By all the usual standards, then, Europeans and most others are acting as if they resent some aspects of U.S. policy, are irritated by America's influence, oppose selected actions the administration has taken, and dislike President Bush more than his predecessor, but remain entirely unthreatened by the United States. Of course, it is always possible, as some argue, that balancing behavior against the United States might emerge sluggishly. But if it is unfair to look so soon for hard evidence of balancing, then it is also too soon to conclude that America's post-9/11 foreign policy has overreached. Instead of the verdict's being in, and favoring the administration's critics, the jury is still out. There is no persuasive evidence that U.S. policy is provoking the seismic shift in America's reputation that Bush's critics detect. For now, claiming to detect balancing is the analytic equivalent of shooting from the hip.

If the jury is still out, shouldn't we err on the side of caution? Not if doing so means we are so constrained by multilateralism that we deny ourselves the tools we need to protect ourselves effectively. The possible nexus—made far more imaginable by 9/11—between international terrorist groups and rogue states bent on developing weapons of mass destruction means we are in the unhappy position of asking which risks we should run, not whether we should run any at all.

What the uncertain evidence *does* invite us to do is keep an eye on real benchmarks for detecting possible overreach: credible indicators of balancing behavior against us by other countries. Watching what people do and not simply what they say—even to pollsters—remains the best test of what people really think of America.

10

Jealousy of U.S. Power Causes European Anti-Americanism

Joshua Muravchik

Joshua Muravchik is a resident scholar at the American Enterprise Institute, a Washington, D.C., think tank dedicated to preserving the foundations of freedom.

Many Europeans are anti-American because of their jealousy and fear of America's superpower status. They have made unfounded and irrational complaints against America's actions in the war on terror and other international conflicts. While America's foreign policy is carried out with the intent of making the world safer for everyone, Europe's foreign policy, above all else, appears to be based on jealousy of America's success, and primarily designed to limit the power of the United States.

In response to the attacks of September 11, 2001, German chancellor Gerhard Schroeder promised "unlimited solidarity" with the United States. A year later, he won a second term by pledging to German voters his unconditional refusal to cooperate with America's war against terrorism.

When the World Trade towers crumbled, France's *Le Monde* [newspaper] proclaimed in a banner headline, "We Are All Americans." On the anniversary, the author of those words—French commentator Jean-Marie Colombani—offered a revision: "We have all become anti-Americans."

Joshua Muravchik, "The European Disease: Irrational Anti-Americanism Takes Root Across the Atlantic," *The American Enterprise*, vol. 13, December 2002, pp. 24–28.

The moment at which Europe's solidarity with the United States evaporated came just four months after September 11, when the Pentagon released photos of al-Qaeda prisoners handcuffed and blindfolded as they arrived at a makeshift U.S. prison in Guantanamo [Cuba]. "Tortured" screamed the headline of the *London Mail*. America was slaking its "thirst for revenge," intoned Germany's *Der Spiegel*. Spain's *El Mundo* said Guantanamo reminded it "of the torture centers in Eastern Europe during the Cold War." And former Anglican envoy Terry Waite, invoking his five years of mistreatment at the hands of Islamic fundamentalists in Lebanon, declaimed: "I can recognize the conditions that prisoners are being kept in at Guantanamo Bay because I have been there."

London *Evening Standard* columnist A.N. Wilson argued that, "These stories and pictures horrify us, but they should not surprise us." After all, "the Bush administration . . . are the most merciless exponents of world capitalism, with the determination to have a McDonald's and a Starbucks . . . in every country on earth." (And how better to spread restaurant franchises than by torturing Arabs in Cuba?) The Guantanamo photos, in short, inspired Europe to revert to the hostility toward America that had prevailed for a decade. The outpouring of empathy inspired by the collapse of New York's Twin Towers had only seemed to change all that.

Unfounded complaints

It quickly turned out that the prisoners in the photograph were only shackled and blindfolded because they were being transported. When delegations from the Red Cross and the French and British governments visited Guantanamo, they discovered that the detainees "had absolutely no complaints about mistreatment at all." Yet even after learning that the tales of mistreatment were false, the European parliament adopted a resolution gratuitously calling on the U.S. "to guarantee humane treatment for all detainees . . . and respect for international humanitarian law and human rights norms and principles." Moreover, the oft-repeated complaint that the U.S. was flouting the Geneva convention[1] ignored both the letter and the spirit of that treaty. It allowed many different kinds of fighters

---

1. The Geneva Convention establishes international conventions for the treatment of prisoners of war.

to be considered POWs [prisoners of war], including guerrillas, provided that they carry arms openly and "conduct . . . their operations in accordance with the laws and customs of war." No Archimedean lever could shoehorn al-Qaeda into this definition since the [terrorist] group's very raison d'etre was to erase the most fundamental law of war, the distinction between combatants and non-combatants.

> *The recent message to America from her European allies has been: damned if you do, and damned if you don't.*

Giving the Guantanamo detainees POW status to which they were not entitled would have barred the U.S. from asking them anything other than their names, ranks, and serial numbers, thereby denying America a vital trove of information about future terror plans and operations. (This, while many Europeans were trying to dissuade the U.S. from military action on the grounds that "intelligence" offered better hope of defeating the terrorists.)

The American "threat"

Shortly after the September 11 attacks, the American ambassador to the European Union had suggested that "this will drive the U.S. and the E.U. together. . . . Our common values will take precedence over . . . the lesser issues on which we have been concentrating in the last couple of years." But this turned out to be an American pipe dream. Once the Taliban [regime in Afghanistan] was overthrown and al-Qaeda rousted from the caves of Tora Bora [Afghanistan], America had gotten its pound of flesh, so far as Europe was concerned. Any measures beyond this would show that it was not the terrorists but America that constituted the real "threat to world peace," as South Africa's Nelson Mandela put it.

President [George W.] Bush had been reviled in Europe from the moment he took office. He was a "serial killer" in the words of French education minister Jack Lang (a reference to executions in Texas while Bush was governor). Italy's *La Repubblica* sniffed that "Texas's 'eternal youngster'" needed to learn "that the world is not his family ranch, full of mustangs to tame with America's lasso."

But if Bush epitomized many of the American traits that European elites hate, he was not the source of the transatlantic split. The 1990s were marked by recurrent expressions of European enmity from the trashing of McDonald's to false accusations of industrial espionage by the CIA to Europe's impassioned campaign against capital punishment in America (Italian cities each "adopted" a death row inmate in Texas). When a gun discharged in a French high school in 1998, ending the life of one of the boys who was playing with it, the French minister of education rushed to the press to denounce the real culprit: America, which he said had contaminated France with its "civilization of violence" spread through movies. When French investigative journalists unearthed evidence of their government's complicity with the genocidal regime in Rwanda, French state officials hinted that the CIA had planted these stories as part of an American plot to supplant French influence in Africa. (Everyone knows how much Americans have lusted for a deeper role in Sierra Leone, the Ivory Coast, and Burundi.)

Europe's contradictory actions

Many of the European complaints seemed disingenuous. During debates over enlargement of NATO [North Atlantic Treaty Organization] by including newly free Iron Curtain countries [countries formerly under Soviet control], our European allies wanted the U.S. to pledge never to use force without the authorization of the U.N. [United Nations] Security Council. This contradicted the U.N. Charter itself, which reserves to each state an "inherent right of individual or collective self-defense." Indeed, no sooner had the Europeans made their clamor over this issue than they joined in war against the Serbs over Kosovo, a war that enjoyed neither the blessing of the Security Council nor any basis in international law.

The real motive behind the misplaced demand for Security Council approval, explained London's *Daily Telegraph*, was "fears in European governments [of] Alliance members tagging along behind American-led foreign-policy initiatives." In other words, the same allies who today are making a fuss about the possibility that America would act "unilaterally" without them, were complaining just a few years ago about the prospect that America would act with them. Likewise, current complaints about

American globalism were preceded in the early Bush months by
hand-wringing over American "isolationism." In short, the recent message to America from her European allies has been:
damned if you do, and damned if you don't.

It is similarly hard to take seriously European indignation
over the death penalty. Most European governments themselves only abolished the practice in the 1970s, '80s, and '90s,
and public opinion surveys show that most of their citizens (if
not the elites) continue to favor capital punishment. In any
case, it is impossible to understand how executions in the
United States rank as an important international human rights
concern in a world rife with torture, concentration camps,
extra-judicial executions, slavery, the treatment of women as
property, and many other depredations of tyranny.

Perhaps the European obsession with American executions
was prompted by a categorical sense of the sanctity of human
life. But if so, how to explain Holland's legalization of euthana-
sia or the permissive abortion laws in several E.U. states? Then
consider France and Britain's realpolitik tilt in favor of the Serbs
while they murdered hundreds of thousands of Bosnians; Bel-
gium's acquiescence and France's ambiguous role in the geno-
cide in Rwanda; or Paris's diplomatic support for Iraq despite
Saddam Hussein's well-documented use of chemical weapons to
kill thousands of Iraqi Kurds. What kind of moral sensitivity is
pierced by the execution of violent convicts (the death of [con-
victed Oklahoma City bomber] Timothy McVeigh was "sad, pa-
thetic, and wrong," pronounced the Council of Europe) but little moved by the slaughter of innocents? If it is capital
punishment itself that is somehow unbearable to contemplate,
why Europe's refusal to sponsor resolutions critical of China in
the U.N. Human Rights Commission? China executes as many
prisoners every week as America does in a year.

Failure to rise above jealousy

Something other than humanitarian conviction was driving
the European campaign against capital punishment in the U.S.
The issue had become, said Italian president Carlo Ciampi in
2000, "a most eloquent signal affirming a European identity."
It was, as Jean-Claude Casanova put it in *Le Monde*, a touch-
stone of Europe's sense of "supériorité morale."

Ironically, September 11 gave Europeans a more genuine way
to demonstrate their moral qualities by rising above petty jeal-

ousies to lock arms with America against a common threat. After the first few hopeful signs, however, many Europeans failed this test. In France, *September 11: The Horrifying Fraud*, a book alleging that the attacks were not carried about by foreigners but by right-wingers within the U.S. government, became, as the *Times* of London reported, "an overnight sensation, rocketing to the top of the charts and breaking the national record for first-month sales held by Madonna's *Sex*."

> *Fully two-thirds of the sample of European elites questioned . . . said their countrymen feel it is 'good for the U.S. to be vulnerable.'*

Nor was the mood much kinder to the U.S. even in England, whose Prime Minister [Tony Blair] made himself America's staunchest ally. The novelist Salman Rushdie, a man of the Left rarely accused of pro-American bias, was moved to write: "Night after night, I have found myself listening to Londoners' diatribes against the sheer weirdness of the American citizenry. The [9/11] attacks on America are routinely discounted. ('Americans care only about their own dead.') American patriotism, obesity, emotionality, self-centeredness: These are the crucial issues."

While many Europeans felt genuine sympathy for America for the wound it had suffered, most, according to a poll commissioned by the German Marshall Fund of the United States and the Chicago Council on Foreign Relations [CFR], believed that it was caused in part by U.S. foreign policy. Fully two-thirds of the sample of European elites questioned by the Pew Research Center said their countrymen feel it is "good for the U.S. to be vulnerable."

Threatened by U.S. power?

What about today's opposition to America's [2003] war with Iraq? That in itself is not tantamount to anti-Americanism. Yet there is something fishy about Europe's stance. German foreign minister Joschka Fischer insists [in 2002] that instead of using force, the "sanctions regime" against Iraq should be "further developed." Yet for years, European leaders have been pushing for easing or eliminating those very sanctions. Likewise, Gerhard

Schroeder first said he would not support the use of military power without the authorization of the U.N. Security Council. Then, as the U.S. drew close to securing such authorization, Schroeder pushed back the goal posts and said he would not support military action even with U.N. support. In short, Europe's proposals for dealing with Iraq seemed designed less to force change in Baghdad than to foment paralysis in Washington.

Europe's slipperiness on Middle East policy can also be seen in the case of Iran. A number of Europeans have argued that Iraq is the wrong target because it is relatively low on the list of state sponsors of terrorism. This might have been a strong argument had it been followed to its logical conclusion, namely, to focus the anti-terror campaign on the likes of Syria, Lebanon, and above all Iran. The Tehran regime—whose proclaimed "basic motto" is "death to America"—has done much over two decades to spread a way of thinking throughout the Muslim world of which September 11 was a logical culmination. There is, moreover, no denying Tehran's own terrorist activities in many venues including Europe. Iranian agents are suspected in murderous attacks in France, Germany, Italy, England, Norway, Turkey, and Switzerland, as well as the United States. Yet Europe's current prescription for Iran is to remove sanctions entirely.

> ❝ [Europeans] are not afraid of America; rather they are wounded in their pride by the vast disparity between their successes and ours. ❞

This June [2002], just as mounting street demonstrations and government repression made it clear that much of the Iranian public has lost patience with the Islamic Republic, the E.U. announced a new drive to expand commerce with the Tehran regime. Trade with Iran "has enormous potential in view of the country's rich endowments of petroleum, natural gas, and minerals, as well as agricultural wealth and industrial potential," burbled the European Commission. While a new E.U.-Iranian trade agreement eventually stalled over political conditions, Germany pushed ahead in August [2002] with its own investment pact with Tehran. "Even at a time when there are some doubts in the region, E.U. countries like Germany stick to their policy of boosting bilateral ties," crowed German economics minister Werner Muller. No scruples about terrorism were mentioned. Remind me again, is it America or Europe that represents amoral capitalism?

Apart from its contradictory proposals for dealing with Iran and Iraq, Europe's other strategy for the war against terrorism is to "eradicate the breeding ground for potential terrorism," as European Commission ambassador Gunter Burghardt put it. This "breeding ground" is defined neither as the hate-spewing theocracy of Iran nor the network of mosques and madrassas [schools] where radical Islam is propagated, but rather poverty, which is said to incite Middle Easterners to become terrorists by the thousands. Quite apart from the fact that the perpetrators of the September 11 attacks were men of comfortable means, the E.U. has already demonstrated the futility of this sort of thinking through its funnelling of 3.5 billion euros to the Palestinian Authority since 1994. That makes "Palestine" the world's leading per capita recipient of foreign aid, yet far from abating, Palestinian terror had crescendoed amidst this largesse.

Europe's approach to "battling" terrorism is so hollow and self-contradictory as to suggest that its real goal is to tie the hands of the United States. Europeans seem to feel more threatened by their superpower ally than by bombmakers. The *New York Times* recently quoted a Parisian scholar specializing in the U.S. who complained that "America has no more enemy. It does what it likes now when it wants. Through NATO it directs European affairs. Before we could say we were on America's side. Now there is no counterbalance."

In a like vein, *Der Spiegel* lamented (back during the Clinton years) that "Americans are acting, in the absence of limits put on them by anybody or anything, as if they own a blank check in their 'McWorld.'" Dominique Moisi, the head of France's leading institute of international affairs, commented recently that European hostility is aimed not at what America does, but at "what America is." But what is America that is so offensive—except a superpower that casts Europe's weakness into high relief?

Jealous of America's success

The German Marshall Fund/Chicago CFR survey asked Europeans whether they would like the E.U. to become a superpower like the United States; 65 percent said yes and 14 percent said no. (Among the French, a whopping 91 percent said yes and only 3 percent no.) But only about half of those who said "yes" were willing to increase defense spending to make it happen. Remarkably, nine out of ten said their goal was to be an equal partner with the U.S., not a competitor. In other words, they are not afraid of America; rather they are wounded in their pride by the vast disparity between their successes and ours.

> *Many Europeans prefer to wallow in resentment. Meanwhile, America goes about the dirty business of making the world safer—for itself, and for them.*

The quest to salvage pride also underlies Europe's adoption of a common currency. The goal, said former French prime minister Lionel Jospin, was to "enable Europe to regain its sovereignty . . . to rebalance the big power blocs." Likewise, Germany's former chancellor Helmut Schmidt predicted with satisfaction that the euro "will change the whole world situation so that the United States can no longer call all the shots." For French foreign minister Hubert Vedrine, the euro was just a first step. "The entire foreign policy of France," he declared, "is aimed at making the world of tomorrow composed of several poles, not just a single one." That makes America foreign policy enemy number one.

Is America a selfish rogue state, as some Europeans have claimed? The U.S. war on terrorism is of course motivated by self-defense, but also by a broad concern for world order. Our determination to take down Saddam Hussein,[2] for which we have been so much criticized on the other side of the Atlantic, is especially public spirited. If Washington were truly selfish, it could strike an easy deal with Saddam: Do what you want in your region, just don't mess with us. That is a deal Saddam would surely take. And he would be happy to sell us oil to fund his local tyranny. But it is a deal America will never offer.

The countries for whom the sole polestar is self-interest are the French and the Russians, whose resistance to war against Iraq flows from their own commercial and diplomatic interests, global security be damned. The same pattern of unprincipled

2. In December 2003, Saddam Hussein was captured by U.S. forces.

selfishness, and sycophancy toward the world's oil-rich Muslim states, led six out of nine E.U. members on the U.N. Human Rights Commission to vote for a resolution this spring [2003] that endorsed suicide bombings as a legitimate form of struggle.

It is also selfishness that lies at the root of Europe's weakness. Collectively, the E.U. states are as wealthy and more populous than the United States. They are potentially more powerful—if they are willing to pay the price of subsuming national egos, trimming welfare states, and bearing risks and burdens far from home. But rather than strive for the best in themselves, many Europeans prefer to wallow in resentment. Meanwhile, America goes about the dirty business of making the world safer—for itself, and for them.

11

British Anti-Americanism Is Not Caused by Jealousy

Mark Thomas

Mark Thomas is a contributing writer for New Statesman, *a weekly newsmagazine based in London.*

British anti-Americanism is not due to jealousy of the United States. Far from being jealous, the British people actually dislike many elements of U.S. culture and are often opposed to U.S. foreign policy. Their anti-Americanism is a result of their anger and revulsion at the actions of the United States, not their desire to be like it.

O ver the past year [2002], Britain has seen such a fantastic increase in anti-Americanism that I really feel there should be prizes, or at least badges, to hand out for this great effort. Not in the old Soviet style of badges of dead politicians' faces; I think it is time for badges of politicians we would like to see dead: like a tie pin with [U.S. vice president] Dick Cheney clutching his chest. Or one of those commemorative plates engraved with [U.S. president George W.] Bush in an autoerotic asphyxiation pretzel incident, toppling, statesmanlike, from the desk in the Oval Office.

A few weeks ago [in July 2002], I appeared on a *Newsnight* debate with William Shawcross, ex–[Vietnamese Communist leader] Ho Chi Min cheerleader and now right-wing man of tweed; and Tom Reid, the European correspondent for the *Wash-*

ington Post. They argued that anti-Americanism is the product of our jealousy of the US. Jealous of what, exactly? Jealous of a political leader who at times can barely string a sentence together? Of course not, we have [British deputy prime minister] John Prescott, for a start. But do we secretly harbour a desire to have a deputy leader who is being investigated by the Securities and Exchange Commission and sued for his time as chief executive and chairman of the Halliburton Company? Do we long for a political system where hoards of MPs [members of Parliament] are financed by a corporation [Enron] that goes belly up after being lied about by its auditors and sucked dry by its directors? If we are jealous of the American way of life, then the anti-American majority in Britain actually craves the highest obesity rate in the world. They want to own handguns and run major sporting events called the World Series without inviting any other country to take part. Our deepest desire must be to see people in Britain paying for private health insurance.

Jealous of America?

Anti-Americanism, according to Shawcross, really comes from the liberal media elite, as if north London is full of Prada-wearing hacks screeching, "Darling, anyone who is anyone simply loathes the Yanks. America is sooo last millennium." But if they, too, are secretly jealous of the US, then [British town] Hampstead can't wait for the reintroduction of the death penalty, or to see channel after channel of screaming TV evangelists calling homosexuals Satan's semen-drenched acolytes. Tom Reid argues that anti-Americanism is the product of European countries no longer having an empire and hating America's superpower status. Surely the anti-war movement doesn't want an empire, nor does it want to kill as many civilians as America does. Frankly, Reid might muster a better argument if he said, "You don't like America because there are two As in the word."

But maybe, Tom and William, we are not jealous of America's continuing economic blockade of Cuba, spitefully held because Cuba had the audacity to defy American plans for the region. And what of the American-led sanctions on Iraq, which have left an American-armed dictator in power while the Iraqi people suffer?[1] Do I wish that Britain had played a bigger role

---

1. Saddam Hussein's government was toppled by the 2003 U.S.-led war on Iraq, and Hussein was captured by the U.S. forces.

in the sanctions that UNICEF [United Nations Children's Fund] estimates have been responsible for the deaths of half a million Iraqi children under five?

What of US military aid to Israel? Surely I should secretly wish that there were more British components in the F-16s [aircraft] that pound the illegally occupied territories. As the Apache attack helicopters carry out their extrajudicial killings and assassinations, I should be sitting in front of the TV news, saying, "If only those were British helicopters killing the Palestinians."

In the politics of the playground, Bush would demand that Palestinians democratically elect someone whom the US wants, and not [Palestinian leader Yasser] Arafat, and the whole of Britain would whine, "Oh, we hated him first and more than what you do." The US gives about $2.5bn [billion] in military aid to Colombia, the country with the worst human rights record in South America. According to Tom and William's theory, we should be trying to outdo America by organising whip-rounds for paramilitary death squads in the local pubs. We should be shaking tins, shouting, "Just 15 [pounds sterling] can pay for enough bullets to wipe out a family of trade unionists. Come on, we can match the Yanks."

Revulsion at America's actions

The father of Colombia's president-elect Uribe Velez was allegedly linked to drug-trafficking. His political secretary and close friend, Pedro Juan Moreno, was found by the US Drug Enforcement Administration to be importing, without a licence, the chemicals used as a precursor to transform coca paste to cocaine. Tom and William would have me wish [British prime minister Tony] Blair financed as many, if not more, "private security operations" for this man as Bush does?

Surely all of the above, plus the International Criminal Court, the UN [United Nations] mission in Bosnia, 6,000 Afghan civilians killed [during the 2001 U.S. invasion of Afghanistan], Kyoto[2] and so on, might just be a clue that envy plays no part in anti-Americanism—and that the real reason is anger and revulsion at the world's biggest rogue state.

---

2. the worldwide agreement to limit emission of greenhouse gases that the United States has not signed

12

Hollywood's Representation of the United States Causes Anti-Americanism

Michael Medved

Michael Medved, author of Hollywood vs. America, *hosts a nationally syndicated daily radio talk show focusing on the intersection of politics and pop culture.*

Hollywood's negative portrayal of American culture has contributed to anti-Americanism around the world. Contrary to popular belief, however, Hollywood's portrayal of America does not reflect reality. While history shows that this distorted portrayal of America is not necessary to Hollywood's success, Hollywood continues to spread misleading views about America, inaccurately emphasizing the dysfunctional elements of American life. This incorrect portrayal has led other nations to believe that Americans are violent, oversexed atheists. By giving a more accurate view of U.S. culture, Hollywood could increase America's worldwide popularity rather than destroy it.

"Think America: Why the whole world hates you?" This message, proudly proclaimed in a hand-lettered sign held aloft by a scowling, bearded Pakistani protestor during one of the angry demonstrations that followed [the September 11, 2001, terrorist attacks] continues to challenge the

Michael Medved, "That's Entertainment? Hollywood's Contribution to Anti-Americanism Abroad," *National Interest*, Summer 2002, pp. 5–15. Copyright © 2002 by *National Interest*. Reproduced by permission.

world's dominant power. In responding to such disturbing questions about the origins of anti-Americanism, glib commentators may cite the imperial reach of U.S. corporations, or Washington's support for Israel, or sheer envy for the freedom and prosperity of American life. But they must also contend with the profound impact of the lurid Hollywood visions that penetrate every society on earth. The vast majority of people in Pakistan or Peru, Poland or Papua New Guinea, may never visit the United States or ever meet an American face to face, but they inevitably encounter images of L.A. and New York in the movies, television programs and popular songs exported everywhere by the American entertainment industry.

Those images inevitably exert a more powerful influence on overseas consumers than they do on the American domestic audience. If you live in Seattle or Cincinnati, you understand that the feverish media fantasies provided by a DMX music video or a *Dark Angel* TV episode do not represent everyday reality for you or your neighbors. If you live in Indonesia or Nigeria, however, you will have little or no first-hand experience to balance the negative impressions provided by American pop culture, with its intense emphasis on violence, sexual adventurism, and every inventive variety of anti-social behavior that the most overheated imagination could concoct. No wonder so many Islamic extremists (and so many others) look upon America as a cruel, Godless, vulgar society—a "Great Satan," indeed.

> **❝** *If you live in Indonesia or Nigeria . . . you will have little or no first-hand experience to balance the negative impressions provided by American pop culture.* **❞**

During violent anti-American riots in October 2001, mobs in Quetta, Pakistan specifically targeted five movie theaters showing U.S. imports and offered their negative review of this cinematic fare by burning each of those theaters to the ground. "Look what they did!" wailed Chaudary Umedali amid the smoking ruins of his cinema. He said that a thousand rioters smashed the doors of his theater and threw firebombs inside because "they didn't like our showing American films." Ironically, the last movie he had offered his Quetta customers was

Desperado—a hyper-violent, R-rated 1995 shoot-em-up with Antonio Banderas and Salma Hayek, specifically designed by its Texas-born director Robert Rodriguez for export outside the United States (in this case, to worldwide Hispanic audiences).

Even the President of the United States worries publicly about the distorted view of this embattled nation that Hollywood conveys to the rest of the world. In his eloquent but uncelebrated address to students at Beijing's Tsinghua University on February 22 [2002], [U.S. president] George W. Bush declared: "As America learns more about China, I am concerned that the Chinese people do not always see a clear picture of my country. This happens for many reasons, and some of them of our own making. Our movies and television shows often do not portray the values of the real America I know."

> ❰❰ Do the dark and decadent images we broadcast to the rest of the world hand a potent weapon to America-haters everywhere? ❱❱

Ironically, the President assumed in his remarks that the Beijing students he addressed felt repulsed by the messages they received from American entertainment—despite abundant evidence that hundreds of millions of Chinese, and in particular the nation's most ambitious young people, enthusiastically embrace our pop culture. During the tragic Tiananmen Square rebellion [in 1989], pro-democracy reformers not only seized on the Statue of Liberty as a symbol of their movement, but indulged their taste for the music and fashions identified everywhere as part of American youth culture. American conservatives may abhor the redoubtable Madonna and all her works, but the youthful activists who brought about the Velvet Revolution in Prague [Czechoslovakia in 1989, which marked the fall of communism there] reveled in her cultural contributions.

This contradiction highlights the major dispute over the worldwide influence of Hollywood entertainment. Do the spectacularly successful exports from the big show business conglomerates inspire hatred and resentment of the United States, or do they advance the inevitable, End-of-History triumph of American values? Does the near-universal popularity of national icons from Mickey Mouse to Michael Jackson represent the power of our ideals of free expression and free markets, or do the dark and decadent images we broadcast to the rest of the world hand a potent weapon to America-haters everywhere?

Telling it like it isn't

Of course, apologists for the entertainment industry decry all attempts to blame Hollywood for anti-Americanism, insisting that American pop culture merely reports reality, accurately reflecting the promise and problems of the United States, and allowing the worldwide audience to respond as they may to the best and worst aspects of our society. During a forum on movie violence sponsored by a group of leading liberal activists, movie director Paul Verhoeven (author of such worthy ornaments to our civilization as *Robocop* and *Basic Instinct*) insisted: "Art is a reflection of the world. If the world is horrible, the reflection in the mirror is horrible." In other words, if people in developing countries feel disgusted by the Hollywood imagery so aggressively marketed in their homelands, then the problem cannot be pinned on the shapers of show business but rather arises from the authentic excesses of American life.

This argument runs counter to every statistical analysis of the past twenty years on the distorted imagery of American society purveyed by the entertainment industry. All serious evaluations of movie and television versions of American life suggest that the pop culture portrays a world that is far more violent, dangerous, sexually indulgent (and, of course, dramatic) than everyday American reality. George Gerbner, a leading analyst of media violence at the Annenberg School of Communications at the University of Pennsylvania, concluded after thirty years of research that characters on network television fall victim to acts of violence at least fifty times more frequently than citizens of the real America.

If anything, the disproportionate emphasis on violent behavior only intensifies with the export of American entertainment. For many years, so-called action movies have traveled more effectively than other genres, since explosions and car crashes do not require translation. This leads to the widespread assumption abroad that the United States, despite the dramatically declining crime rate of the last decade, remains a dangerous and insecure society. On a recent trip to England, I encountered sophisticated and thoughtful Londoners who refused to travel across the Atlantic because of their wildly exaggerated fear of American street crime—ignoring recent statistics showing unequivocally that muggings and assaults are now more common in London than in New York. On a similar note, a recent traveler in rural Indonesia met a ten-year old boy who, discovering the American origins of the visitor, asked to see her gun. When she insisted that she didn't carry any firearms, the child refused to believe her: he knew that all Americans carried guns because he had seen them perpetually armed on TV and at the movies.

> *The misleading media treatment of sexuality has proven . . . unreliable in its oddly altered version of American life.*

The misleading media treatment of sexuality has proven similarly unreliable in its oddly altered version of American life. Analysis by Robert and Linda Lichter at the Center for Media and Public Affairs in Washington, DC, reveals that on television, depictions of sex outside of marriage are nine to fourteen times more common than dramatizations of marital sex. This odd emphasis on non-marital intercourse leads to the conclusion that the only sort of sexual expression frowned upon by Hollywood involves physical affection between husband and wife. In reality, all surveys of intimate behavior (including the famous, sweeping 1994 national study by the University of Chicago) suggest that among the more than two-thirds of American adults who are currently married, sex is not only more satisfying, but significantly more frequent, than it is among their single counterparts. . . .

Anyone acquainted with actual unattached individuals could confirm that [television shows] *Friends* and *Ally McBeal* hardly represent the common lot of American singles. On television and at the movies, the major challenge confronted by most unmarried characters is trying to decide among a superficially dazzling array of sexual alternatives. The entertainments in question may suggest that these explorations will prove less than wholly satisfying, but to most American viewers, single or married, they still look mightily intriguing. To most viewers in more traditional societies, by contrast, they look mightily decadent and disrespectful.

Emphasis on homosexuality

Consider, too, the emphasis on homosexuality in contemporary television and movies. In less than a year between 2001 and 2002, three major networks (NBC, HBO, MTV) offered different, competing dramatizations of the murder of Matthew Shepherd—the gay Wyoming college student beaten to death by two thugs. No other crime in memory—not even the murder of Nicole Brown Simpson—has received comparable attention by major entertainment companies. The message to the world at large not only calls attention to homosexual alternatives in American life, but focuses on our brutal and criminal underclass.

The Gay and Lesbian Alliance Against Defamation (GLAAD) publishes an annual scorecard in which it celebrates the number of openly gay characters who appear regularly on national television series, and recently counted more than thirty. This trendy fascination with homosexuality (as illustrated by the worshipful attention given to Rosie O'Donnell's hugely publicized "coming out") obviously overstates the incidence of out-of-the-closet gay identity; all scientific studies suggest that less than 3 percent of adults unequivocally see themselves as gay.

> *Church or synagogue attendance . . . hardly ever appears in Hollywood or television portrayals of contemporary American society.*

For purposes of perspective, it is useful to contrast the pop culture focus on gay orientation with media indifference to religious commitment. A handful of successful television shows such as *Touched by an Angel* and *7th Heaven* may invoke elements of conventional faith, if often in simplistic, childlike form, but ardent and mature believers remain rare on television and at the movies. The Gallup Poll and other surveys suggest that some 40 percent of Americans attend religious services on a weekly basis—more than four times the percentage who go to the movies on any given week. Church or synagogue attendance, however, hardly ever appears in Hollywood or television portrayals of contemporary American society, while mass media feature gay references far more frequently than religious ones. This is hardly an accurate representation of mainstream America, and the distortion plays directly into the hands of some of our most deadly enemies. In October 2001, an "official" press spokesman for Osama bin Laden's Al-Qaeda terror network summarized the struggle between Islamic fanatics and the United States as part of the eternal battle "between faith and atheism." Since the United States represents by far the most religiously committed, church-going nation in the Western world, this reference to the nation's godlessness gains credibility abroad only because of Hollywood's habitual denial or downplaying of the faith-based nature of our civilization.

The ugly media emphasis on the dysfunctional nature of our national life transcends examples of widely decried, tacky and exploitative entertainment, and pointedly includes the most prodigiously praised products of the popular culture. In recent years, some 1.5 billion people around the world watch at least part of Hollywood's annual Oscar extravaganza, and in April 2000 they saw the Motion Picture Academy confer all of its most prestigious awards (Best Picture, Best Actor, Best Director, Best Screenplay) on a puerile pastiche called *American Beauty*. This embittered assault on suburban family life shows a frustrated father (Kevin Spacey) who achieves redemption only through quitting his job, lusting after a teenaged cheerleader, insulting his harridan wife, compulsively exercising and smoking marijuana. The only visibly loving and wholesome relationship in this surreal middle class nightmare flourishes between two clean-cut gay male neighbors. The very title, *American Beauty*, ironically invokes the name of an especially cherished flower to suggest that all is not, well, rosy with the American dream. If the entertainment establishment chooses to honor this cinematic effort above all others, then viewers in Kenya or Kuala Lumpur might understandably assume that it offers a mordantly accurate assessment of the emptiness and corruption of American society. . . .

Why do they watch it?

The question remains: Why does so much of the world still seem so single-mindedly obsessed with American entertainment, for all its chaotic and unrepresentative elements?

The most likely answer involves what might be described as the "*National Enquirer* appeal" of Hollywood's vision of life in the United States. While waiting in the supermarket checkout lines, we turn to the scandal-ridden tabloids not because of our admiration for the celebrities they expose, but because of our uncomfortable combination of envy and resentment toward them. The tabloids compel our attention because they allow us to feel superior to the rich and famous. For all their wealth and glamor and power, they cannot stay faithful to their spouses, avoid drug addiction, or cover up some other guilty secret. We may privately yearn to change places with some star of the moment, but the weekly revelations of the *National Enquirer* actually work best to reassure us that we are better off as we are.

> **//** *Violent, demented, anti-social and conspiratorial thinking has come to characterize a major segment of the entertainment establishment.* **//**

In much the same way, Hollywood's unpleasant images of America enable the rest of the world to temper inevitable envy with a sense of their own superiority. The United States may be rich in material terms (and movies and television systematically overstate that wealth), but the violence, cruelty; injustice, corruption, arrogance and degeneracy so regularly included in depictions of American life allow viewers abroad to feel fortunate by comparison. Like the *Enquirer* approach to the private peccadilloes of world-striding celebrities, you are supposed to feel fascinated by their profligate squandering of opportunity and power. . . .

This love-hate relationship with Hollywood's twisted imagery also characterized the 19 conspirators who made such a notable attempt to "destroy evil America" with their September 11 [2001] atrocities. During their months and years in the United States, Mohammed Atta and his colleagues savored the popular culture—renting action videos and visiting bars, peep shows, lap dancing parlors and Las Vegas—immersing themselves in Western degradation to stiffen their own hatred (and self-hatred?) of it.

Recognizing the influence of Hollywood

In response to the terrorist attacks and to the onset of the war that followed, leaders of the Hollywood community expressed some dawning awareness that they may have indeed contributed to some of the hatred of America expressed around the world. Beyond a brief flurry of flag-waving, and the generous contributions to the 9/11 fund by leading celebrities from Julia Roberts to Jim Carrey, members of the entertainment elite showed a new willingness to cooperate with the defense establishment. Working through the Institute for Creative Technologies at USC [University of Southern California] (originally created to enlist Hollywood talent for shaping virtual reality simulators for military training), creators of movies like *Die Hard, Fight Club* and even *Being John Malkovich* brainstormed with Pentagon brass. Their purpose, according to several press reports, involved an attempt to concoct the next possible plot that might be launched against the United States, and then to devise strategies to counteract it.

In a sense, this unconventional program acknowledged the fact that violent, demented, anti-social and conspiratorial thinking has come to characterize a major segment of the entertainment establishment. How else could an objective observer interpret the idea that the military turned first to millionaire screenwriters in order to understand the thought processes of mass-murdering terrorists? . . .

A plea to Hollywood

In his February [2002] speech in Beijing, President Bush held the Chinese students transfixed with a picture of America that departed dramatically from the visions they had received from made-in-USA music, movies and television. "America is a nation guided by faith", the President declared. "Someone once called us 'a nation with the soul of a church.' This may interest you—95 percent of Americans say they believe in God, and I'm one of them." Bush went on to appeal to the family priorities that have characterized Chinese culture for more than 3,000 years: "Many of the values that guide our life in America are first shaped in our families, just as they are in your country. American moms and dads love their children and work hard and sacrifice for them because we believe life can always be better for the next generation. In our families, we find love and learn responsibility and character."

If Hollywood's leaders placed themselves within the context of the wider American family, they might also learn responsibility and character—and discover that a more wholesome, loving and balanced portrayal of the nation they serve could enhance rather than undermine their worldwide popularity.

13

A Fear of Modernism Results in Anti-Americanism

Fouad Ajami

Fouad Ajami is a professor at Johns Hopkins University's School of Advanced International Studies and a contributing editor at U.S. News & World Report.

Polls show that global anti-Americanism is increasing. Much of the worldwide hatred directed at the United States is actually a reaction against the forces of modernism, which America represents. To many countries, America's modern culture is highly desirable, yet at the same time it is perceived as a threat to an old way of life. Thus, America is in the inescapable position of being loved and hated at the same time.

Pollsters report rising anti-Americanism worldwide. The United States, they imply, squandered global sympathy after the September 11 [2001] terrorist attacks through its arrogant unilateralism. In truth, there was never any sympathy to squander. Anti-Americanism was already entrenched in the world's psyche—a backlash against a nation that comes bearing modernism to those who want it but who also fear and despise it.

Italian novelist Ignazio Silone once observed it. It is in Karachi and Paris, in Jakarta and Brussels. An idea of it, a fantasy of it, hovers over distant lands. And everywhere there is also an obligatory anti-Americanism, a cover and an apology for the spell the United States casts over distant peoples and places. In the burning grounds of the Muslim world and on its periphery, U.S. embassies and their fate in recent years bear witness to a duality of the United States as Satan and redeemer. The embassies targeted by the masters of terror and by the diehards are besieged by visa-seekers dreaming of the golden, seductive country. If only the crowd in Tehran offering its tired rhythmic chant "marg bar amrika" ("death to America") really meant it! It is of visas and green cards and houses with lawns and of the glamorous world of Los Angeles, far away from the mullahs and their cultural tyranny, that the crowd really dreams. The frenzy with which radical Islamists battle against deportation orders from U.S. soil—dreading the prospect of returning to Amman and Beirut and Cairo—reveals the lie of anti-Americanism that blows through Muslim lands.

> *Anti-Americanism [is] . . . a backlash against a nation that comes bearing modernism to those who want it but who also fear and despise it.*

The world rails against the United States, yet embraces its protection, its gossip, and its hipness. Tune into a talk show on the stridently anti-American satellite channel Al-Jazeera, and you'll behold a parody of American ways and techniques unfolding on the television screen. That reporter in the flak jacket, irreverent and cool against the Kabul or Baghdad background, borrows a form perfected in the country whose sins and follies that reporter has come to chronicle.

In Doha, Qatar, Sheik Yusuf al-Qaradawi, arguably Sunni Islam's most influential cleric, at Omar from al-Khattab Mosque, a short distance away from the headquarters of the U.S. Central Command, delivers a khutba, a Friday sermon. The date is June 13, 2003. The cleric's big theme of the day is the arrogance of the United States and the cruelty of the war it unleashed on Iraq [in 2003]. This cleric, Egyptian born, political to his fingertips, and in full mastery of his craft and of the sensibility of his followers, is particularly agitated in his sermon. Surgery and a period of recovery have kept him away from his pulpit for three months, during which time there has been a big war in the Arab world that toppled Saddam Hussein's regime in Iraq with stunning speed and effectiveness. The United States was "acting like a god on earth," al-Qaradawi told the faithful. In Iraq, the United States had appointed itself judge and jury. The invading power may have used the language of liberation and enlightenment, but this invasion of Iraq was a 21st-century version of what had befallen Baghdad in the middle years of the 13th century, in 1258 to be exact, when Baghdad, the city of learning and culture, was sacked by the Mongols.

> **"** *To come bearing modernism to those who want it but who rail against it at the same time . . . is the American burden.* **"**

The preacher had his themes, but a great deal of the United States had gone into the preacher's art: Consider his Web site, Qaradawi.net, where the faithful can click and read his fatwas (religious edicts)—the Arabic interwoven with HTML text—about all matters of modern life, from living in non-Islamic lands to the permissibility of buying houses on mortgage to the follies of Arab rulers who have surrendered to U.S. power.

Or what about his way with television? He is a star of the medium, and Al-Jazeera carried an immensely popular program of his. That art form owes a debt, no doubt, to the American "televangelists," as nothing in the sheik's traditional education at Al Azhar University in Cairo prepared him for this wired, portable religion. And then there are the preacher's children: One of his daughters had made her way to the University of Texas where she received a master's degree in biology, a son had earned a Ph.D. from the University of Central Florida in Orlando, and yet another son had embarked on that quintessential American degree, an MBA at the American University in Cairo. Al-Qaradawi embodies anti-Americanism as the flip side of Americanization.

Anti-Americanism around the world

Of late, pollsters have come bearing news and numbers of anti-Americanism the world over. The reports are one dimensional and filled with panic. This past June [2002] the Pew Research Center for the People and the Press published a survey of public opinion in 20 countries and the Palestinian territories that indicated a growing animus toward the United States. In the same month, the BBC [British Broadcasting Corporation] came forth with a similar survey that included 10 countries and the United States. On the surface of it, anti-Americanism is a river overflowing its banks. In Indonesia, the United States is deemed more dangerous than [the terrorist group] al Qaeda. In Jordan, Russia, South Korea, and Brazil, the United States is thought to be more dangerous than Iran, the "rogue state" of the mullahs.

There is no need to go so far away from home only to count the cats in Zanzibar. These responses to the United States are neither surprising nor profound. The pollsters, and those who have been brandishing their findings, see in these results some verdict on the Bush presidency—but the findings could be read as a crude, admittedly limited, measure of the foul temper in some unsettled places. The pollsters have flaunted spreadsheets to legitimize a popular legend: It is not Americans that people abroad hate, but the United States! Yet it was Americans who fell to terrorism on September 11, 2001, and it is of Americans and their deeds, and the kind of social and political order they maintain, that sordid tales are told in Karachi and Athens and Cairo and Paris. You can't profess kindness toward Americans while attributing the darkest of motives to their homeland.

> **//** *The United States is destined to be in the politics—and imagination—of strangers even when the country (accurately) believes it is not implicated in the affairs of other lands.* **//**

The Pew pollsters ignored Greece, where hatred of the United States is now a defining feature of political life. The United States offended Greece by rescuing Bosnians and Koso-vars. Then, the same Greeks who hailed the Serbian conquest of Srebrenica in 1995 and the mass slaughter of the Muslims there were quick to summon up outrage over the U.S. military campaign in Iraq. In one Greek public opinion survey, Americans were ranked among Albanians, Gypsies, and Turks as the most despised peoples. . . .

Beyond the Yugoslav wars, the neo-Orthodox worldview sanctified the ethnonationalism of Greece, spinning a narrative of Hellenic persecution at the hands of the United States as the standard-bearer of the West. Greece is part of NATO [North Atlantic Treaty Organization] and of the European Union (EU), but an old schism—that of Eastern Orthodoxy's claim against the Latin world—has greater power and a deeper resonance. In the banal narrative of Greek anti-Americanism, this animosity emerges from U.S. support for the junta that reigned over the country from 1967 to 1974. This deeper fury enables the aggrieved to glide over the role the United States played in the defense and rehabilitation of Greece after World War II. Furthermore, it enables them to overlook the lifeline that migration offered to untold numbers of Greeks who are among the United States' most prosperous communities.

Greece loves the idea of its "Westernness"—a place and a culture where the West ends, and some other alien world (Islam) begins. But the political culture of religious nationalism has isolated Greece from the wider currents of Western liberalism. What little modern veneer is used to dress up Greece's anti-Americanism is a pretense. The malady here is, paradoxically, a Greek variant of what plays out in the world of Islam: a belligerent political culture sharpening faith as a political weapon, an abdication of political responsibility for one's own world, and a search for foreign "devils.". . .

We were all Americans

The introduction of the Pew report sets the tone for the entire study. The war in Iraq, it argues, "has widened the rift between Americans and Western Europeans" and "further inflamed the Muslim world." The implications are clear: The United States was better off before [George W.] Bush's "unilateralism." The United States, in its hubris, summoned up this anti-Americanism. Those are the political usages of this new survey.

But these sentiments have long prevailed in Jordan, Egypt, and France. During the 1990s, no one said good things about the United States in Egypt. It was then that the Islamist children of Egypt took to the road, to Hamburg [Germany] and Kandahar [Afghanistan], to hatch a horrific conspiracy against the United States. And it was in the 1990s, during the fabled stock market run, when the prophets of globalization preached the triumph of the U.S. economic model over the protected versions of the market in places such as France, when anti-Americanism became the uncontested ideology of French public life. Americans were barbarous, a threat to French cuisine and their beloved language. U.S. pension funds were acquiring their assets and Wall Street speculators were raiding their savings. The United States incarcerated far too many people and executed too many criminals. All these views thrived during a decade when Americans are now told they were loved and uncontested on foreign shores. . . .

The burden of modernity

To come bearing modernism to those who want it but who rail against it at the same time, to represent and embody so much of what the world yearns for and fears—that is the American burden. The United States lends itself to contradictory interpretations. To the Europeans, and to the French in particular, who are enamored of their *laicisme* (secularism), the United States is unduly religious, almost embarrassingly so, its culture suffused with sacred symbolism. In the Islamic world, the burden is precisely the opposite: There, the United States scandalizes the devout, its message represents nothing short of an affront to the pious and a temptation to the gullible and the impressionable young. According to the June [2003] BBC survey, 78 percent of French polled identified the United States as a "religious" country, while only 10 percent of Jordanians endowed it with that label. Religious to the secularists, faithless to the devout—such is the way the United States is seen in foreign lands.

So many populations have the United States under their skin. Their rage is oddly derived from that very same attraction. Consider the Saudi realm, a place where anti-Americanism is fierce. The United States helped invent the modern Saudi world. The Arabian American Oil Company—for all practical purposes a state within a state—pulled the desert enclave out of its insularity, gave it skills, and ushered it into the 20th century. Deep inside the anti-Americanism of today's Saudi Arabia, an observer can easily discern the dependence of the Saudi elite on their U.S. connection. It is in the image of the United States' suburbs and urban sprawl that Saudi cities are designed. It is on the campuses of [American universities] Harvard, Princeton, and Stanford that the ruling elite are formed and educated.

After September 11, 2001, the Saudi elite panicked that their ties to the United States might be shattered and that their world would be consigned to what they have at home. Fragments of the United States have been eagerly embraced by an influential segment of Saudi society. For many, the United States was what they encountered when they were free from home and family and age-old prohibitions. Today, an outing in Riyadh is less a journey to the desert than to the mall and to Starbucks.

An academic in Riyadh, in the midst of an anti-American tirade about all policies American, was keen to let me know that his young son, born in the United States, had suddenly declared he no longer wanted to patronize McDonald's because of the United States' support of Israel. The message was plaintive and unpersuasive; the resolve behind that "boycott" was sure to crack. A culture that casts so long a shadow is fated to be emulated and resented at the same time. The United States is destined to be in the politics—and imagination—of strangers even when the country (accurately) believes it is not implicated in the affairs of other lands.

> *Modernism is frightening. It means we have to compete. It means we can't explain everything away with conspiracy theories.*

In a hauntingly astute set of remarks made to the *New Yorker* in the days that followed the terrorism of September 11, the Egyptian playwright Ali Salem—a free spirit at odds with the intellectual class in his country and a maverick who journeyed to Israel and wrote of his time there and of his acceptance of that country—went to the heart of the anti-American phenomenon. He was thinking of his own country's reaction to the United States, no doubt, but what he says clearly goes beyond Egypt:

> People say that Americans are arrogant, but it's not true. Americans enjoy life and they are proud of their lives, and they are boastful of their wonderful inventions that have made life so much easier and more convenient. It's very difficult to understand the machinery of hatred, because you wind up resorting to logic, but trying to understand this with logic is like measuring distance in kilograms. . . . These are people who are envious. To them, life is an unbearable burden. Modernism is the only way out. But modernism is frightening. It means we have to compete. It means we can't explain

everything away with conspiracy theories. [Writer] Bernard Shaw said it best, you know. In the preface to 'St. Joan,' he said Joan of Arc was burned not for any reason except that she was talented. Talent gives rise to jealousy in the hearts of the untalented. . . .

Disturbance of the modern

A century ago, in a short-story called "Youth," the great British author Joseph Conrad captured in his incomparable way the disturbance that is heard when a modern world pushes against older cultures and disturbs their peace. In the telling, Marlowe, Conrad's literary double and voice, speaks of the frenzy of coming upon and disturbing the East. "And then, before I could open my lips, the East spoke to me, but it was in a Western voice. A torrent of words was poured into the enigmatical, the fateful silence; outlandish, angry words mixed with words and even whole sentences of good English, less strange but even more surprising. The voice swore and cursed violently; it riddled the solemn peace of the bay by a volley of abuse. It began by calling me Pig. . . ."

Today, the United States carries the disturbance of the modern to older places—to the east and to the intermediate zones in Europe. There is energy in the United States, and there is force. And there is resistance and resentment—and emulation—in older places affixed on the delicate balancing act of a younger United States not yet content to make its peace with traditional pains and limitations and tyrannies. That sensitive French interpreter of his country, Dominique Moisi, recently told of a simple countryman of his who was wistful when [Iraqi leader] Saddam Hussein's statue fell on April 9 [2003 at the conclusion of the war in Iraq] in Baghdad's Firdos Square. France opposed this war, but this Frenchman expressed a sense of diminishment that his country had sat out this stirring story of political liberation. A society like France with a revolutionary history should have had a hand in toppling the tyranny in Baghdad, but it didn't. Instead, a cable attached to a U.S. tank had pulled down the statue, to the delirium of the crowd. The new history being made was a distinctly American (and British) creation. It was soldiers from [American cities] Burlington, Vermont, and Linden, New Jersey, and Bon Aqua, Tennessee—I single out those towns because they are the hometowns of three soldiers who were killed in the Iraq war—who raced through the desert making this new history and paying for it.

The United States need not worry about hearts and minds in foreign lands. If Germans wish to use anti-Americanism to absolve themselves and their parents of the great crimes of World War II, they will do it regardless of what the United States says and does. If Muslims truly believe that their long winter of decline is the fault of the United States, no campaign of public diplomacy shall deliver them from that incoherence. In the age of Pax Americana, it is written, fated, or maktoob (as the Arabs would say) that the plotters and preachers shall rail against the United States—in whole sentences of good American slang.

Organizations to Contact

The editors have compiled the following list of organizations concerned with the issues debated in this book. The descriptions are derived from materials provided by the organizations. All have publications or information available for interested readers. The list was compiled on the date of publication of the present volume; names, addresses, phone and fax numbers, and e-mail addresses may change. Be aware that many organizations take several weeks or longer to respond to inquiries, so allow as much time as possible.

American Enterprise Institute (AEI)
1150 17th St. NW, Washington, DC 20036
(202) 862-5800 • fax: (202) 862-7177
e-mail: info@aei.org • Web site: www.aei.org

The American Enterprise Institute for Public Policy Research is a scholarly research institute that is dedicated to preserving a strong foreign policy and national defense. Its publications include articles in its magazine *American Enterprise* and books including *Study of Revenge: The First World Trade Center Attack and Saddam Hussein's War Against America* and *An End to Evil: How to Win the War on Terror*. Articles, speeches, and seminar transcripts on American foreign relations are available on its Web site.

Brookings Institution
1775 Massachusetts Ave. NW, Washington, DC 20036
(202) 797-6000 • fax: (202) 797-6004
e-mail: brookinfo@brook.edu • Web site: www.brookings.org

The Brookings Institution is a think tank that conducts research and education in foreign policy, economics, government, and the social sciences. Its Saban Center for Middle East Policy develops programs to promote a better understanding of policy choices in the Middle East. Articles on American foreign relations can be found on the organization's Web site and in its publications including the quarterly *Brookings Review*.

Cato Institute
1000 Massachusetts Ave. NW, Washington, DC 20001-5403
(202) 842-0200 • fax: (202) 842-3490
e-mail: cato@cato.org • Web site: www.cato.org

The Cato Institute is a libertarian public policy research foundation dedicated to limiting the role of government and promoting free markets and peace. It disapproves of an interventionist foreign policy and believes that the use of U.S. forces in other countries should be limited. The institute publishes the quarterly magazine *Regulation*, the bimonthly *Cato Policy Report*, and numerous papers dealing with foreign policy, including "The Empire Strikes Out: The 'New Imperialism' and Its Fatal Flaws," and "Did U.S. Intervention Overseas Breed Terrorism?"

Center for Strategic and International Studies (CSIS)
1800 K St. NW, Suite 400, Washington, DC 20006
(202) 887-0200 • fax: (202) 775-3199
Web site: www.csis.org

The center works to provide world leaders with strategic insights and policy options on current and emerging global issues. It publishes books including *The "Instant" Lessons of the Iraq War*; the *Washington Quarterly*; a journal on political, economic, and security issues; and other publications including reports that can be downloaded from its Web site.

Council on Foreign Relations
58 E. 68th St., New York, NY 10021
(212) 434-9400 • fax: (212) 986-2984
e-mail: communications@cfr.org • Web site: www.cfr.org

The council specializes in foreign affairs and studies the international aspects of American political and economic policies and problems. Its journal *Foreign Affairs*, published five times a year, includes analyses of America's relations with countries around the world.

Foreign Policy Association (FPA)
470 Park Ave. South, 2nd Fl., New York, NY 10016
(212) 481-8100 • fax: (212) 481-9275
e-mail: info@fpa.org • Web site: www.fpa.org

FPA is a nonprofit organization that believes a concerned and informed public is the foundation for an effective foreign policy. Publications such as the annual *Great Decisions* briefing book and the quarterly *Headline Series* review U.S. foreign policy issues in China, the Persian Gulf and the Middle East, and Africa.

Heritage Foundation
214 Massachusetts Ave. NE, Washington, DC 20002
(202) 546-4400 • fax: (202) 546-8328
e-mail: info@heritage.org • Web site: www.heritage.org

The Heritage Foundation is a conservative public-policy research institute. Its position papers and reports on America's foreign policy include "Turning Back the Terrorist Threat: America's Unbreakable Commitment," "Forging a Durable Post-War Political Settlement in Iraq," and "The Future of Transatlantic Relations."

Hoover Institution
Stanford University, Stanford, CA 94305-6010
(650) 723-1754 • fax: (650) 723-1687
e-mail: horaney@hoover.stanford.edu
Web site: www-hoover.stanford.edu

The Hoover Institution is a public-policy research center devoted to advanced study of politics, economics, and international affairs. It publishes the quarterly *Hoover Digest* and *Policy Review*—which often includes articles on American foreign relations—as well as a newsletter and special reports including "Foreign Policy for America in the Twenty-first Century."

Institute for Policy Studies (IPS)
733 15th St. NW, Suite 1020, Washington, DC 20005
(202) 234-9382 • fax: (202) 387-7915
Web site: www.ips-dc.org

The Institute for Policy Studies is a progressive think tank that works to develop societies built around the values of justice and nonviolence. It publishes reports including *Global Perspectives: A Media Guide to Foreign Policy Experts*. Numerous articles and interviews on September 11, 2001, and terrorism are available on its Web site.

Iraq Action Coalition
7309 Haymarket Ln., Raleigh, NC 27615
fax: (919) 846-7422
e-mail: iac@leb.net • Web site: www.iraqaction.org

The Iraq Action Coalition is an online media and activists' resource center for groups and activists who opposed both international economic sanctions and U.S. military action against Iraq. It publishes books and reports on Iraq including *Iraq Under Siege: The Deadly Impact of Sanctions and War*. Its Web site includes numerous links to other organizations opposed to the war against Iraq.

Middle East Forum
1500 Walnut St., Suite 1050, Philadelphia, PA 19102
(215) 546-5406 • fax: (215) 546-5409
e-mail: info@meforum.org • Web site: www.meforum.org

The Middle East Forum is a think tank that works to define and promote American interests in the Middle East. It supports strong American ties with Israel, Turkey, and other democracies as they emerge. It publishes the *Middle East Quarterly*, a policy-oriented journal. Its Web site includes articles, summaries of activities, and a discussion forum.

Middle East Institute
1761 N St. NW, Washington, DC 20036-2882
(202) 785-1141 • fax: (202) 331-8861
e-mail: mideasti@mideasti.org
Web site: www.themiddleeastinstitute.org

The institute's charter mission is to promote better understanding of Middle Eastern cultures, languages, religions, and politics. It publishes numerous books, papers, audiotapes, and videos as well as the quarterly *Middle East Journal*. It also maintains an educational outreach department to give teachers and students of all grade levels advice on resources.

Middle East Media Research Institute (MEMRI)
PO Box 27837, Washington, DC 20038-7837
(202) 955-9070 • fax: (202) 955-9077
e-mail: memri@memri.org • Web site: www.memri.org

MEMRI translates and disseminates articles and commentaries from Middle East media sources and attempts to increase understanding between the West and the Middle East.

Middle East Policy Council
1730 M St. NW, Suite 512, Washington, DC 20036-4505
(202) 296-6767 • fax: (202) 296-5791
e-mail: info@mepc.org • Web site: www.mepc.org

The Middle East Policy Council was founded in 1981 to expand public discussion and understanding of issues affecting U.S. policy in the Middle East. The council is a nonprofit educational organization that operates nationwide. It publishes the quarterly *Middle East Policy Journal*.

Middle East Research and Information Project (MERIP)
1500 Massachusetts Ave. NW, Washington, DC 20005
(202) 223-3677 • fax: (202) 223-3604
e-mail: ctoensing@merip.org • Web site: www.merip.org

MERIP is a nonprofit, nongovernmental organization with no links to any religious, educational, or political organizations in the United States or elsewhere. Its mission is to educate the public about the contemporary Middle East with particular emphasis on U.S. foreign policy, human rights, and social justice issues. It publishes the bimonthly *Middle East Report*.

Trilateral Commission
345 E. 46th St., New York, NY 10017
(212) 661-1180 • fax: (212) 949-7268
e-mail: trilat@panix.com • Web site: www.trilateral.org

The commission encourages shared leadership responsibilities among the countries in North America, Western Europe, and Japan. It publishes the annual magazine *Trialogue* and the report "Addressing the New International Terrorism: Prevention, Intervention, and Multilateral Cooperation."

United Nations (UN)
UN Headquarters
First Avenue at 46th St., New York, NY 10017
Web site: www.un.org

The UN is an international organization dedicated to maintaining international peace and security, developing friendly relations among nations, and promoting international cooperation. Articles and speeches about American foreign relations are available on its Web site.

Washington Institute for Near East Policy
1828 L St. NW, Suite 1050, Washington, DC 20036
(202) 452-0650 • fax: (202) 223-5364
e-mail: info@washingtoninstitute.org
Web site: www.washingtoninstitute.org

The institute is an independent, nonprofit research organization that provides information and analysis on the Middle East and U.S. policy in the region. It publishes numerous books; periodic monographs; and reports on regional politics, security, and economics, including *Peace-Watch*, which focuses on the Arab-Israeli peace process; and other reports including "Democracy and Arab Political Culture" and "Radical Middle East States and U.S. Policy."

Bibliography

Books

Daniel Byman and Matthew C. Waxman — *Confronting Iraq: U.S. Policy and the Use of Force Since the Gulf War*. Santa Monica, CA: RAND, 2000.

Noam Chomsky — *Hegemony or Survival: America's Quest for Global Dominance (The American Empire Project)*. New York: Metropolitan, 2003.

Richard Crockatt — *America Embattled: September 11, Anti-Americanism, and the Global Order*. New York: Routledge, 2003.

Noah Feldman — *After Jihad: America and the Struggle for Islamic Democracy*. New York: Farrar, Straus and Giroux, 2003.

Daniel J. Flynn — *Why the Left Hates America: Exposing the Lies that Have Obscured Our Nation's Greatness*. Roseville, CA: Forum, 2002.

Peter Hays Gries — *China's New Nationalism: Pride, Politics, and Diplomacy*. Berkeley: University of California Press, 2004.

Fred Halliday — *Two Hours That Shook the World: September 11, 2001: Causes and Consequences*. London: Saqi, 2002.

Chalmers Johnson — *Blowback: The Costs and Consequences of American Empire*. New York: Metropolitan, 2000.

Robert Kagan — *Of Paradise and Power: America and Europe in the New World Order*. New York: Knopf, 2003.

Douglas Kellner — *From 9/11 to Terror War: The Dangers of the Bush Legacy*. Lanham, MD: Rowman & Littlefield, 2003.

Samuel S. Kim, ed. — *Korea's Democratization*. Cambridge, NY: Cambridge University Press, 2003.

Gabriel Kolko — *Another Century of War?* New York: New Press, 2002.

Michael Mandelbaum — *The Ideas That Conquered the World: Peace, Democracy, and Free Markets in the Twenty-First Century*. New York: PublicAffairs, 2002.

Alan L. McPherson — *Yankee No!: Anti-Americanism in U.S.–Latin American Relations*. Cambridge, MA: Harvard University Press, 2003.

131

Michael Moore   *Dude, Where's My Country?* New York: Warner Books, 2003.

Walter Mosley   *What Next: A Memoir Toward World Peace.* Baltimore: Black Classic, 2003.

Joseph S. Nye Jr.   *The Paradox of American Power: Why the World's Only Superpower Can't Go It Alone.* New York: Oxford University Press, 2002.

George Packer, ed.   *The Fight Is for Democracy: Winning the War of Ideas in America and the World.* New York: Perennial, 2003.

Jean-François Revel   *Anti-Americanism.* Trans. Diarmid Cammell. San Francisco: Encounter, 2003.

William Shawcross   *Allies: The U.S., Britain, and Europe, and the War in Iraq.* New York: PublicAffairs, 2004.

Periodicals

Fouad Ajami   "The Falseness of Anti-Americanism," *Foreign Policy*, September/October 2003.

Conrad Black   "Counsel to Britain: U.S. Power, the 'Special Relationship' and the Global Order," *National Interest*, Fall 2003.

Ed Blanche   "Brothers in Arms? An Old Arab Proverb Notes: My Brother and Me Against My Cousin, My Cousin and Me Against the Stranger," *Middle East*, December 2003.

Anthony J. Blinken   "The False Crisis over the Atlantic," *Foreign Affairs*, May/June 2001.

James W. Caeser   "A Genealogy of Anti-Americanism," *Public Interest*, July 23, 2003.

Christopher Caldwell   "No, Europe Needs to Get Real: To This American, It's Europeans Who Are Naïve, Superficial, and Materialistic," *Time International*, January 20, 2003.

J.D. Considine   "An American in Canada: For the Record, I Don't Believe You All Hate Me. And I Know All About Bluster," *Maclean's*, April 7, 2003.

Reginald Dale   "European Union, Properly Construed," *Policy Review*, December 2003/January 2004.

Jean Daniel   "Our American 'Enemies,'" *World Press Review*, December 2003.

Shelley Delos   "A Dim View: The World Looks at Bush," *Political Affairs*, December 2003.

John Derbyshire   "Yearning to Be Liked," *New Criterion*, November 2003.

Economist	"Against America? Moi? France's Diplomacy," March 15, 2003.
Economist	"The Distance of Neighbors; Latin America and the United States," April 19, 2003.
Jeffrey Fields	"Is It Necessarily Bad?" *Humanist*, November/December 2002.
Leon T. Hadar	"Mending the U.S-European Rift over the Middle East," *Cato Policy Analysis*, August 20, 2003.
Robin Harris	"The State of the Special Relationship," *Policy Review*, June/July 2003.
Stanley Hoffman	"Why Don't They Like Us? How America Has Become the Object of Much of the Planet's Genuine Grievances—and Displaced Discontents," *American Prospect*, November 19, 2001.
Llewellyn D. Howell	"The French: Rivals, but Not Enemies," *USA Today Magazine*, July 2003.
International Economy	"Why Does the World Hate America?" Winter 2003.
Boris Johnson	"Bush Is Leading the U.S. to Tragedy: The Saudi Ambassador Tells Boris Johnson That America Is Hated and War on Iraq Is Mad," *Spectator*, September 7, 2002.
Paul Johnson	"To Hate America Is to Hate Humanity," *Spectator*, April 6, 2002.
Robert Kagan	"Power and Weakness," *Policy Review*, June/July 2003.
Charles W. Kegley Jr. and Gregory A. Raymond	"Preemptive War: A Prelude to Global Peril?" *USA Today*, May 2003.
Richard Lambert	"Misunderstanding Each Other," *Foreign Affairs*, March/April 2003.
Christopher Layne	"Casualties of War: Transatlantic Relations and the Future of NATO in the Wake of the Second Gulf War," *Cato Policy Analysis*, August 13, 2003.
Dmitry Marin	"Why Do They Hate Us?" *Political Affairs*, December 2003.
Jessica T. Matthews	"Estranged Partners," *Foreign Policy*, November/December 2001.
David Moberg	"The Road from Baghdad," *In These Times*, May 5, 2003.
Moises Naim	"The Perils of Anti-Americanism: Why Knee-Jerk Criticism of the United States Carries Dangerous Hidden Costs," *Foreign Policy*, May/June 2003.

Michael Neumann   "Anti-Americanism: Too Much of a Good Thing?"
                           Counterpunch, September 13, 2003.

New Statesman   "Proud to Be Anti-American?" November 17, 2003.

Eric Pape   "Stay at Home, Europe," *Newsweek International*,
                           July 28, 2003.

Owen Rathbone   "Poland: A True Friend of America," *American
                           Daily*, May 4, 2003.

Matthew Rothschild   "Bush Trashes the United Nations," *Progressive*,
                          April 2003.

Simon Schama   "The Unloved American," *New Yorker*, March 10,
                          2003.

Tim Shorrock   "A Dangerous Game in Korea; U.S. Policies Are
                          Fanning Anti-Americanism in Both the North and
                          the South," *Nation*, January 27, 2003.

Andrew Sullivan   "Hating America," *American Enterprise*, April/May
                          2003.

John M. Swomley   "The Ultimate Rogue Nation," *Humanist*, January/
                          February 2001.

Jay Tolson   "Separated by More than an Ocean," *U.S. News &
                          World Report*, March 10, 2003.

Steven Vincent   "Baghdad, with Victims," *Commentary*, December
                          2003.

Paul Michael Wihbey   "The End of the Affair: Paul Michael Wihbey Pre-
                          dicts a Total Collapse of the Long-Standing Rela-
                          tionship Between the United States and Saudi Ara-
                          bia," *Spectator*, September 6, 2003.

Phil Zabriskie   "Diminished Expectations: For Many Asians,
                          America No Longer Stands for Peace, Freedom, and
                          Liberty," *Time International*, April 7, 2003.

Index